Adventures in Chicken

Adventures in Chicken

150 Amazing Recipes from the

Creator of AdventuresInCooking.com

Eva Kosmas Flores

Houghton Mifflin Harcourt
Boston New York 2016

A Hollan Publishing, Inc. Concept

For information about permission to reproduce selections
from this book, write to trade.permissions@hmhco.com
or to Permissions, Houghton Mifflin Harcourt Publishing
Company, 3 Park Avenue, 19th Floor, New York,
New York 10016.

www.hmhco.com

Library of Congress Cataloging-in-Publication Data
Names: Flores, Eva Kosmas, author.

Title: Adventures in chicken / Eva Kosmas Flores.

Description: Boston : Houghton Mifflin Harcourt, 2016. |
Includes index.

Identifiers: LCCN 2015038041| ISBN 9780544558205
(paper over board) | ISBN 9780544558212 (ebook)

Subjects: LCSH: Cooking (Chicken) | LCGFT: Cookbooks.

Classification: LCC TX750.5.C45 F597 2016 | DDC
641.6/65 — dc23

LC record available at http://lccn.loc.gov/2015038041

Designed by Jan Derevjanik

Printed in China

TOP 10 9 8 7 6 5 4 3 2 1

To my best friend and husband, Jeremy.

"When someone asks what there is to do,
light the candle in his hand.
Like this." —Rumi

CONTENTS

ACKNOWLEDGMENTS

A HUGE THANK YOU TO JUSTIN SCHWARTZ, Cynthia Brzostowski, and the rest of the team over at Houghton Mifflin Harcourt for making this book happen, and thank you to my agent Holly Schmidt and everyone at Hollan Publishing for all of their hard work. A very dear thank you to my husband for trying such a massive amount of chicken dishes without complaint, and for tidying up the kitchen after my daily whirlwind through it. Thank you to my mother for helping me with recipe testing and being the best "assistant mom" ever, and to both my parents for always believing in me. Thank you to Sasha Swerdloff and Lindsey Saletta for lending their hands in the kitchen and in front of the camera. And a huge thank you to my dear friend Carey Nershi, who is always there when I need her.

INTRODUCTION

"When I write of hunger, I am really writing about love and the hunger for it, and warmth and the love of it and the hunger for it...and then the warmth and richness and fine reality of hunger satisfied...and it is all one."
—M.F.K. FISHER

AS I WRITE THIS, I AM WATCHING MY EIGHT small chicks skittering about their brooder. They tilt their heads one way and another, pecking along the ground through their pine shaving bedding, scratching aggressively at the bottom of the box, as if they'll unearth a worm underfoot if they just dig deep enough. This instinct follows through to the wild adult chicken, whose diet of a wide variety of bugs and seeds requires consumption of sand and grit in the form of tiny pebbles eaten off the ground, which then reside in its stomach and help it break down all the nutty and tasty shelled bits it forages for. At six days old, my chicks weigh less than a small muffin, but in a few months' time, they'll be nearly full-grown. Their breasts will become plump and their leg quarters will fill out with dark-flushed tendons. They'll be rid of their downy fluff and grow long, conspicuous feathers. And in about six months they'll begin laying their eggs. Yes, I have adopted these hens to give me a constant supply of eggs rather than a brief supply of meat, but in this short time, they have already impressed me with their vigor, adaptability, and gumption.

Chickens are one of a few varieties of flightless birds. Unable to flap their wings to gain flight for more than a few seconds at a time, their limited mobility and diminutive size unintentionally categorized them as the perfect domesticated bird, staying put in even the most rudimentary coops. Inexpensive to raise, they will forage on whatever bugs, nuts, seeds, fruit, and/or vegetables come across their habitat. With the current backyard chicken phenomenon, there are complex concoctions of pre-mixed nuts and seeds you can feed your bird to ensure complete nutritional consumption, but in most parts of the world where raising large and demanding livestock is not an option, chickens are the primary source of meat. These adaptable creatures do not require acres of pasture, nor do they require mounds of specialized grasses. They can live in a variety of climates and locations and can forage for much of their diet if given access to the proper landscape (i.e., one with bugs, seeds, and/or vegetables around). This ability to adapt, survive, and even thrive in such a wide variety of landscapes is what has brought the chicken to the forefront of every culture's cuisine.

From the coq au vin of France, to the chicken fricassee of Cuba, to the pad thai of Thailand, every corner of the earth has adapted several cherished preparations of this flightless bird, each one more different and intriguing than the next. On its own, roasted without seasoning, chicken has a very mild, savory, and lightly buttery flavor that intensifies when you go from the light meat to the dark. But once you incorporate spices, sauces, fruits, vegetables, or herbs, choose from roasting, braising, grilling, simmering, or frying, and then get down to the specific part of the

chicken, whether the juicy drumsticks, the crispy wings, or perhaps the whole bird spatchcocked and flattened, you end up with a staggering and never-ending array of equally sumptuous dishes.

In Thailand, ground chicken and sweet Thai basil leaves are stir-fried together in a hot wok with a variety of regional sauces. In Tennessee, Hot Chicken is a popular present-day preparation that entails deep-frying various chicken parts and serving them atop slices of plain fluffy white bread adorned with homemade pickles. In Peru, the most common dish is *pollo a la Brasa,* in which a whole chicken is salted, skewered, and cooked over hot coals. And in Greece, the bird is most often roasted with lemons, onions, garlic, oregano, olive

oil, and potatoes, a method my father learned from his parents many years ago on the small island of Aegina, where my *yiayia* and *papou* tended to their own flock of poultry. Papou was a shoemaker and pistachio farmer, and Yiayia, having eight children on a farm on a rural Greek island, worked full time making sure everyone was fed, clothed, and had a clean place to sleep. Their home consisted of three rooms, the kitchen/master bedroom, the dining room, and the children's bedroom. Money, as you can imagine, was not something that was in excess. But, having a coop of chickens provided a reliable source of low-fat and high-protein sustenance for the growing family. And even in the dry, arid, and rocky island climate, the birds were happy to eat any scraps, bugs, and seeds tossed their way (my father recalls that they were particularly fond of melon rinds).

The enjoyment of chickens, however, hasn't been limited to the diets of the poor. They have been relished by queens, captains, sultans, and leaders of nations alike throughout the entirety of their existence. A palate for chicken, it seems, does not distinguish between the rich and the poor, but only between those with and without functioning taste buds. The chicken, in its adaptable and easygoing fashion, has provided both wealthy and impoverished peoples with a reliable food source for hundreds if not thousands of years. And it is because of this duality that there is such a staggering array of ways to prepare this delightfully simple creature.

Being asked to develop 150 recipes with the same key ingredient at first seemed like a markedly strenuous task. But the more I spoke to friends and family about their favorite preparations, the less difficult it became. And then, I started speaking to complete strangers about it. Inquiring into the minds of acquaintances about their beloved chicken dishes not only provided me with a bottomless reservoir of inspiration, but it also created a bond over a simple love of food. Every single person had at least one cherished dish to talk about, with the vast majority of them coming from their families and cultures, providing a glimpse into the life and story behind each person: who they are, where they came from, who the primary cook in their family was, and why they love that particular preparation of this humble bird so much. Sometimes it was because of the surroundings in which they ate it, whether in their mother's home or during a faraway holiday celebration. Other times it was because it reminded them of the person who made it, some of whom were no longer a part of this world. And just as often, it was simply because it tasted really, really good.

So, when reading this book, I ask you to consider the chicken. Consider it as not only a meal, but as a bridge between cultures, beliefs, and people. And consider it as it truly is, a remarkably adaptable living creature that has a right to a comfortable existence, no matter its final resting place or the brevity of its life. And so, it is in this way that I hope this book gives you the urge not to simply eat to get by, sprinkling a boneless skinless chicken breast with salt, pan-frying it, and calling it dinner, but to eat to explore, inquire, bond, and most importantly, to savor the sensual miracle that is the art of eating.

Why Pastured Poultry?

There are many benefits to eating exclusively pastured chickens, but first I want to talk a little bit about what pastured poultry means, particularly in comparison to "free range" and standard high-density confinement chickens. The USDA regulations for free range poultry require that the bird has access to the outdoors; they do not,

however, define the amount of time the bird has that access, the necessary size or population density of the outdoor area, or the plant materials available for grazing in the space. So theoretically, a poultry farm could have a 10,000-square-foot indoor barn and a 50-square-foot fenced-in outdoor gravel area with an open entryway between the two areas allowing chickens to pass in and out for 15 minutes a day and qualify as free range.

Most commercially available chickens come from high-density confinement poultry farms, which is where a large number of chickens are crowded and raised together. Some are raised in cages, but even with the label "cage-free," the poultry can still be confined to an indoor structure where they are all crowded together on the floor. Chickens are inherent grazers and have evolved to wander around an open environment and peck at the ground for food. Crowding them all together to the point where they can't walk around can cause an increase in cannibalism, where they peck at each other to the point of injury and death. To help prevent this from happening, some of these high-density confinement farms clip the ends of the chickens' beaks so that they cannot peck each other but can still eat and drink. This is more common in egg-laying poultry facilities than in meat-processing ones, since broiler chickens are usually slaughtered before adult aggression sets in. Some broiler chickens develop breasts so heavy that they cannot stand for very long because their legs have not evolved to the point where they can support the new weight of their body, so they are unable to move very much, if at all.

As you can imagine, high-density facilities tend to have more issues with bacterial infections because of the large numbers of chickens defecating in a confined and crowded space. To counteract this, many chickens are supplied with a dose of antibiotics. Now, the pro and con

Cutting a Whole Chicken into Individual Parts

To cut up a whole chicken, first remove the wishbone: Lift up the flap of skin over the neck area so you can see the exposed muscle. Cut a V-shape about ½ inch below the neck, going about 1 inch deep. Reach in with your thumb and forefingers and feel around for the bone. Once you locate it, position your thumb behind the center of the wishbone and push it forward until you can get a grip on it with both the thumb and forefinger, then pull it out.

Remove the wings by cutting through the joint on the wing where it attaches to the body. Set the wings aside.

Remove the legs by holding one leg above the chicken so that the weight of the chicken is hanging from it. Cut along the skin attaching the leg to the breast; as you cut the skin will pull apart and display the muscle and sinew. Pull the leg back towards the back of the chicken to pop the leg joint out of the socket; you will hear a small crack once it happens. Now cut underneath the leg muscle that extends into the back (this area is known as the "oyster"). Lay the leg tucked up against the bird and then fold it over so the top of the leg is now facing the bottom of the bird. Cut through the exposed sinews and the leg should come off easily. Repeat with the other leg.

To remove the breasts, lay the chicken breast facing up. Make a clean cut down the center of the chicken, cutting around both sides of the protruding sternum. Lay the chicken on its side and feel for the joint towards the top of the breast near where the wing attaches. Once you locate it, cut under it with your knife to sever its connection to the spine. Use one hand to hold down the chicken's body, grab the entire breast with the other hand, and pull it down off the chicken. Set it aside and repeat with the other breast.

Lay the bird flat on its back. You should see two small fillets of meat still attached to the breast area on either side of the sternum. Grab them at the thickest part and pull them off in a downward motion.

You have now broken down a chicken. While you may be tempted to just toss the carcass after you are finished, don't. The flavor in the bones and joints make for excellent chicken stock. If you don't have time to make stock right away, place the carcass in a freezer-safe resealable container and keep it in the freezer. Use it to make stock within 6 months.

Spatchcocking

Spatchcocking a chicken flattens the bird by removing the backbone, breaking the breastplate, and unfolding it to lay it flat. This helps the chicken cook more quickly and evenly, and exposes more skin, which crisps up the entire bird quite nicely. This is a great cooking technique if you'd like to prepare a whole chicken at once but don't have a lot of time on your hands, since it significantly reduces the cooking time, and also allows you to grill the entire chicken over a gas or charcoal grill, since it allows the entire surface of the flattened bird to be exposed to the heat at once. (*Butterflying* is another term that's often used interchangeably with spatchcocking, and through all my research on the subject I wasn't able to find a definitive difference between the two methods, which both involve removing the backbone to allow the chicken to lay flat.)

To spatchcock a chicken, lay it on its breast so that the back is facing up. Using a very sharp pair of kitchen shears, cut along one side of the backbone, cutting as close to it as you can without

actually cutting the backbone itself. Cut along the other side of the backbone until it is separate from the bird. The backbone can be saved and used for chicken stock or discarded.

Flip the bird over so that the breast is facing up and the back muscles are splayed out on either side of the breast. Press down firmly on the breast of the bird with the heel of your hand to break and flatten the breast bone. To ensure even cooking with the new shape of the chicken, lift up the wing and make a small ¾-inch-wide and 1-inch-deep incision into the joint. Repeat with the other wing and both leg joints. The incisions should not be visible from the top of the bird since they're underneath each of the appendages. The incisions allow more heat into those areas of the bird that tend to take longer to cook, thus ensuring that the breast meat doesn't get overcooked while you're waiting for the thigh meat to finish.

If you're grilling the chicken rather than roasting it, push two long skewers through the chicken to form an X-shape, inserting each into a leg quarter and exiting through the opposite upper corner of the breast. Repeat the same technique on the left breast and right thigh of the chicken. This helps maintain the shape of the chicken and makes it easier to flip the chicken over while you're grilling it without the bird flopping around as much.

Trussing

Trussing the bird helps keep the chicken from drying out while cooking. Crossing the legs over the entry point of the cavity crates a seal that keeps in moisture, which rises to the top of the cavity, condenses, and then runs back down the sides of the ribcage, essentially creating a self-basting steam room of flavor inside the bird. Without crossing and tying the legs over the entry point of the cavity, the steam is able to escape and the chicken dries out much more quickly.

Before trussing and roasting the chicken, you might want to remove the wishbone (see page 17) as it makes for easier carving of the breast meat later on.

To truss the bird, lay it breast side up and slide the cooking twine just underneath the back of the chicken so that it lies directly underneath the leg joints. Cross the twine over the top of the chicken so that it falls directly over the legs. Place the twine that is now looping around back to the back of the chicken underneath the drumsticks on either side and pull to tighten and close. Bring the twine over the wings and around them to the back of the bird and secure with a tight knot.

Tenting

Tenting tinfoil over the chicken's roasting pan helps keep moisture inside the bird and is the best method to ensure that the bird doesn't brown too quickly. The tenting step is especially important in glazes with a high sugar content, as the sugar can crystallize and burn easily without proper tenting. To tent a chicken, take a large sheet of tinfoil about 4 times the size of the pan and fold in half to create a thick double layer of tinfoil. Then fold that slightly in half so that it creates what looks like a camping tent. Place the tent over the bird and secure it onto the edges of the pan by pressing to seal it. Fold the open side at each end shut to seal in the chicken. Poke a small 1-inch hole in the tent to allow excess steam to escape. Make sure the tent does not touch the actual skin of the bird, otherwise it will cook onto it and tear the skin off when you remove the foil.

variety of cuts and make it easier to defrost only what you need, I recommend breaking down some of the birds (see page 17) and then separating them out into 1 pound servings of like-cuts in freezer-safe resealable plastic bags. So for example, if I bought a dozen chickens, I would leave three whole so I had a few whole chickens for roasting and spatchcocking, and the rest I would break down and have 1 pound bags of chicken thighs, 1 pound bags of chicken drumsticks, 1 pound bags of chicken breasts, and so on.

To avoid freezer burn, you want to minimize the chicken's exposure to air. The easiest way to do this is to double wrap each cut of chicken in plastic wrap before placing it in the freezer-safe resealable plastic bag. Once you have 1 pound of cuts in the bag and are ready to seal it, press as much air as possible out of the bag and seal tightly to ensure no air gets back in. Keeping your freezer's temperature constant and below 0 degrees Fahrenheit will also reduce the effect of freezer burn, as will reducing the amount of time the chicken is in the freezer in the first place, so make sure to label the resealable bags properly with the contents and the date it was frozen. That way you can make sure you're using the oldest items first.

When you freeze a chicken and then thaw it out, it changes the texture of the meat and make it a bit drier and less firm-feeling. This is because the liquid inside of the protein in the chicken expands when it is frozen, and can puncture through the cell walls. When thawed, those punctured cells leak out moisture and can make the bird look a bit deflated in addition to drying it out. So generally speaking, fresh meat makes for a juicier bird than frozen meat, but the cooking technique of course has a large effect on the juiciness and flavor of the final dish, too, so don't swear off frozen chicken completely. You can still have a delicious piece of

chicken regardless of if it was frozen or not.

If you're using frozen chicken, make sure to thaw it completely before cooking, because the cooking instructions given in this cookbook apply to fresh chicken. Using partially frozen chicken will result in an undercooked dish that isn't safe to eat.

Fresh Chicken

Fresh chicken meat should not be cooked or frozen after the use-by date on the package. Chicken meat that has spoiled has a slightly fruity, unpleasant smell to it, and the liquid around and on the bird and meat will be thicker, slimier, and can develop a yellowish tinge to it. If you're going to prepare the chicken near the date of expiration and it smells unpleasantly fruity, it's better to be safe and toss the chicken in favor of buying a newer, fresher cut of meat.

Storing Chicken

Cooked chicken can be safely stored in the refrigerator in an airtight container for 3 to 4 days, but if you prepared a whole bird that was stuffed, make sure to remove and store the stuffing separately, otherwise the internal temperature of the chicken might remain too high and allow bacteria to grow.

Hock Locks

And just a short word about hock locks, which you usually find on turkeys but are also on chickens from time to time. They're the hard plastic locks that bind the drumsticks of the bird together, essentially pre-trussing the bird for you. The hock lock is safe to use in the oven (it won't melt), however I find them to be a bit of an eyesore, so even if I am planning on roasting the whole bird, I remove them and truss the bird myself with cooking twine.

So there you have it, all the little tips and tricks to safely and deliciously preparing a chicken. Now comes the fun part, where you get to put all this newfound knowledge to use. Onwards, to the kitchen!

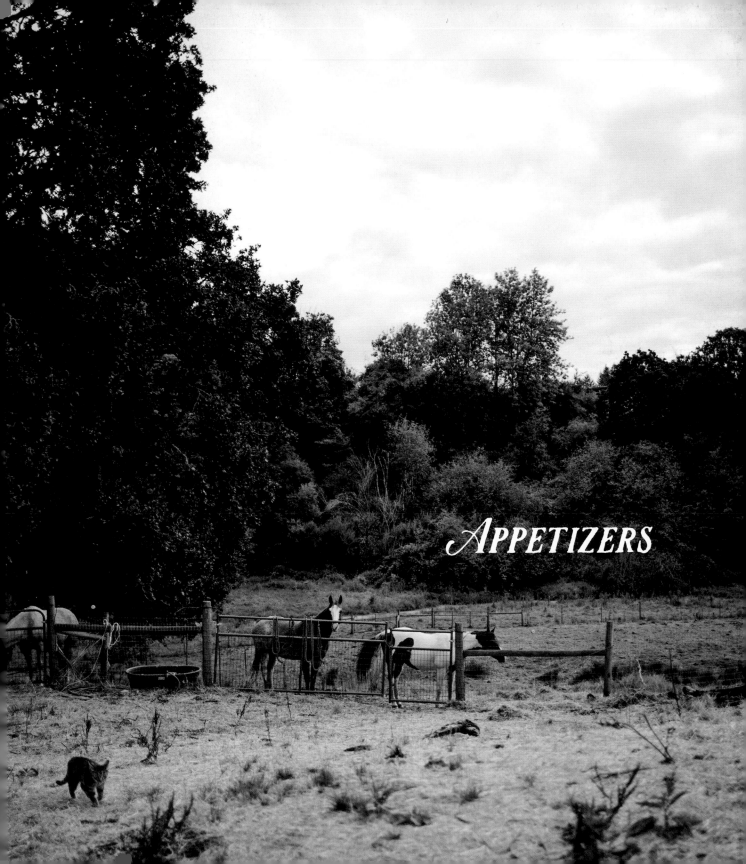

APPETIZERS

CHICKEN CRACKLING CROSTINI
with Maple–Sea Salt Butter

Maple–Sea Salt Butter

4 tablespoons unsalted butter, softened

2½ teaspoons pure maple sugar

¾ teaspoon flaked sea salt

Crostini

1 (4-inch) wide baguette, cut into 12 (½-inch-thick) slices

Chicken skin from 2 leg and thigh pieces, cut into 12 (2-inch) squares

1½ teaspoons finely minced fresh rosemary leaves

½ teaspoon finely minced fresh thyme leaves

½ teaspoon flaked sea salt

¼ teaspoon freshly cracked black pepper

Vegetable oil, for frying

12 fresh sage leaves

6 dates, cut in half lengthwise with pits removed

Pure maple syrup, for serving (optional)

PORK CRACKLINGS ARE A POPULAR SNACK throughout the southern United States, but often forgotten are the equally delicious chicken cracklings. In this recipe, baguette slices spread with a delicious maple and sea salt butter are baked, then topped with crispy pan-fried chicken skin, sweet soft dates, and crispy leaves of sage. The result is the ultimate crunchy, smooth, salty, sweet flavor combination. • makes 12 crostini

Preheat the oven to 400°F.

For the maple butter, in a small bowl, mix together the butter, maple sugar, and sea salt until smooth.

For the crostini, lightly spread the butter mixture across both sides of the 12 baguette slices. Lay the slices flat on a baking sheet, leaving about an inch of space between them. Bake for 12 to 14 minutes, until crisp and golden brown around the edges. Allow to cool completely.

In a bowl, toss the chicken skin with the rosemary, thyme, sea salt, and black pepper until the spices are evenly distributed. Set aside.

Add vegetable oil to a medium frying pan until the oil is about ½ inch deep. Heat the pan over medium heat until a drop of water flicked into the pan sizzles and hisses. Reduce the heat to medium low and add the chicken skin pieces, one at a time, until you can't add any more while maintaining 2 inches of space around each piece. Fry until the skin pieces turn golden brown, 5 to 8 minutes. Remove with a slotted spoon or tongs and place the pieces on a plate lined with paper towels. Repeat until all of the chicken skin has been fried, leaving the reserved oil in the pan.

Add the sage leaves to the same pan, one at a time, making sure to keep the leaves from touching one another. Fry each leaf until crispy, 15 to 30 seconds, then remove with a mesh or slotted spoon and place on a plate lined with paper towels.

To assemble, place a date half on one of the baked baguette slices and press down gently to flatten the date a bit. Place a crispy sage leaf on top of the date and place a chicken crackling on top of the sage leaf. Drizzle with a small spoonful of pure maple syrup to finish, if desired. Repeat with the remaining baked baguette slices, dates, crispy sage, and chicken cracklings until all the crostinis have been assembled and then serve immediately.

Apricot and Rosemary Chicken Salad

There's nothing quite like a fresh chicken salad at a summer barbecue. It cools the mouth between those spicy bites of BBQ and has the most wonderful creamy texture, accented by the occasional crunch of fresh celery. This one incorporates ripe apricots, for a little bit of a sweet-and-sour kick. The key to the rich flavor of the chicken is to cook the breasts with the bone in and skin on so the flavors from the skin and bones seep into the meat while cooking. And even though the bone and skin are discarded, their rich flavor remains in the salad. • serves 4

2½ pounds chicken breasts (about 2 large), bone in and skin on

1 tablespoon extra virgin olive oil

½ teaspoon kosher salt

1 cup chopped celery

½ cup mayonnaise

1 tablespoon plus 1 teaspoon minced fresh rosemary leaves

¼ teaspoon freshly cracked black pepper

1 cup chopped apricot

Preheat the oven to 350°F.

Rub the chicken with the olive oil and ¼ teaspoon of the salt, place in a casserole, and bake for 1 hour to 1 hour and 15 minutes, until the internal temperature of the chicken is at least 165°F. Let cool until warm enough to handle.

Peel the skin off the chicken and remove the meat from the bone by gently easing your fingers underneath the breast meat to peel it off the bone in one large piece. Cut the breast meat into roughly ½-inch cubes and place in a large bowl. Add the celery, mayonnaise, rosemary, black pepper, and remaining ¼ teaspoon salt and stir until combined. Add the chopped apricot and mix gently so as not to crush until evenly distributed throughout the salad. Serve immediately.

Sweet-and-Sour Fried Chicken Wings

Sweet-and-Sour Sauce

½ cup honey

⅓ cup chicken stock

¼ cup ketchup

¼ cup rice vinegar

2 tablespoons freshly squeezed
  lime juice

4 garlic cloves, minced

1 bell pepper, cut into
  ¼-inch-thick slices

2 green onions, sliced

Chicken Wings

2 cups all-purpose flour

1 cup buttermilk

¾ cup water

1 large egg

½ teaspoon freshly cracked
  black pepper

½ teaspoon onion powder

½ teaspoon garlic powder

Canola oil, for frying

2 pounds chicken wings

THERE'S SOMETHING PARTICULARLY WONDERFUL about the resounding crunch that accompanies a deep-fried chicken wing, especially when it's coated in a homemade sweet-and-sour sauce. The key sweet components in the sauce are honey and ketchup, which play off the tangy vinegar and lime juice. Garlic, sweet bell pepper, and green onions are tossed into the sauce to add a bit of crisp freshness and flavor to this simple and satisfying appetizer. • serves 4

––––––––––––––––––––––

For the sweet-and-sour sauce, in a medium saucepan over medium heat, mix together the honey, chicken stock, ketchup, rice vinegar, lime juice, and garlic. Bring to a boil, then add the bell pepper and green onions, reduce the heat, and simmer for 3 minutes. Let cool while you prepare the chicken.

For the chicken wings, in a large bowl, whisk together the flour, buttermilk, water, egg, black pepper, onion powder, and garlic powder. Set aside.

Add canola oil to a large pot until it is 4 inches deep. Heat the oil over medium heat until it reaches 360°F. Pat the chicken wings dry with a paper towel. In batches if necessary to avoid crowding, dip the wings in the batter and use tongs to gently place them in the frying oil. Fry until golden and cooked through, 7 to 8 minutes. Remove the chicken wings with tongs and place on a plate lined with paper towels. Make sure the temperature is back up to 360°F before frying the next batch.

When all the wings are fried, toss with the sweet-and-sour sauce and serve immediately.

SQUASH BLOSSOMS STUFFED
with Chicken and Ricotta

1 tablespoon extra virgin olive oil

1 large shallot, chopped

1 garlic clove, minced

1 pound ground chicken

1 cup chopped cremini mushrooms

1 cup quality whole-milk ricotta cheese

¾ teaspoon kosher salt

¼ teaspoon rubbed dried sage

¼ teaspoon freshly cracked black pepper

About 12 large fresh squash blossoms, pesticide free

Canola oil, for frying

¾ cup all-purpose flour

1 large egg, beaten

DURING THE SUMMER MONTHS EVERY SQUASH VARIETY, whether a zucchini or a straightneck, will produce dozens upon dozens of large golden blossoms. These blooms are one of the largest edible flower varieties in the world, and their firm petals and sturdy base make them perfect for stuffing and pan-frying. These squash blossoms are stuffed with ground chicken that's been sautéed with cremini mushrooms and mixed up with deliciously creamy fresh ricotta cheese. The result is a wonderful rich and savory blossom, filled to the brim with flavor and incredibly beautiful to boot. • makes 12 stuffed squash blossoms

Heat the olive oil, shallot, and garlic in a large frying pan over medium heat, stirring occasionally, for 3 minutes. Add the ground chicken and cook, breaking it apart with the end of your stirring spoon, until nearly cooked through, 6 to 8 minutes. Add the mushrooms and continue cooking, stirring occasionally, until the chicken is cooked through and the mushrooms have browned, 7 to 10 minutes. Let cool before draining the excess oils and liquids from the pan.

Empty the ground chicken mixture into a large bowl. Add the ricotta, ¼ teaspoon of the salt, the sage, and black pepper and mix until combined. Use a tablespoon to scoop a heaping spoonful of the mixture into each squash blossom until about two-thirds full. Fold the last third of the petals over the filling and press down gently to seal.

Add canola oil to a large frying pan until the oil is about 1 inch deep. Heat the oil to 375 degrees Fahrenheit and maintain the temperature throughout frying.

In a medium shallow dish, mix together the flour and remaining ½ teaspoon salt. Lightly brush the outside of each squash blossom with the whisked egg and then roll the blossom in the flour mixture, shaking it gently afterwards to remove any excess flour. Repeat until the squash blossoms are all lightly floured.

In batches if necessary, use a slotted spoon to add the blossoms, one at a time, to the frying pan, maintaining an inch of space around each one. Cook until lightly golden, 3 to 5 minutes on each side. Remove with a slotted spoon and place on a plate lined with paper towels to absorb any excess oil. Serve immediately.

Pesto Chicken Bruschetta

I COULDN'T STOP EATING THESE ONCE THEY WERE DONE, there's just something about the crunchy bits of pan-fried pancetta on top of an herbed pan-fried chicken breast, fresh pesto, Parmesan cheese, and tomato-grated toast. Yep, you basically make toast and scrape a cut tomato across the top so the soft pulp of the tomato is encased in the stiff air pockets of the toast, softening it slightly and leaving behind a deliciously concentrated, fresh tomato flavor. These guys are perfect for entertaining as they make a stunning presentation, and taste just as good as they look. • makes about 14 bruschetta

3 tablespoons extra virgin olive oil

4 ounces pancetta, cut into ½-inch cubes

½ pound boneless skinless chicken breast (about 1)

½ teaspoon kosher salt

½ teaspoon freshly cracked black pepper

½ teaspoon dried basil

1 thin baguette, cut into 14 (½-inch-thick) slices

3 small ripe tomatoes

½ cup pesto (see page 207), or store-bought

2 ounces thickly shaved Parmesan cheese

Preheat the oven to 375°F.

Heat 1 tablespoon of the olive oil in a small frying pan over medium-high heat. Add the pancetta and cook, stirring occasionally, until lightly crispy, about 4 minutes. Remove the pancetta with a slotted spoon and set aside on a plate lined with paper towels.

Coat the chicken with the salt, pepper, and basil. Place in the oil remaining in the frying pan and cook over medium heat until lightly golden on both sides and cooked through, 6 to 7 minutes per side. Remove from the pan and set aside to cool. Cut the chicken into 1-inch-thick strips that are roughly 3 inches in length.

Use a pastry brush to brush the remaining 2 tablespoons olive oil onto the baguette slices. Arrange them in a flat even layer on a baking sheet and bake for about 15 minutes, until lightly toasted and golden around the edges.

Cut 1 of the tomatoes in half and gently scrape the exposed side against the tops of the warm toasted bread. Dice the remaining tomatoes and set aside.

Spread about 1 heaping tablespoon of the pesto across each baguette and place a Parmesan shaving on top. Place a chicken strip on the Parmesan and sprinkle with a generous pinch of the pancetta and diced tomatoes. Serve immediately.

Mediterranean Chicken and Hummus Toasts

Hummus

3 (15-ounce) cans garbanzo
  beans, drained and rinsed

1 cup extra virgin olive oil

10 garlic cloves, peeled

¼ cup freshly squeezed lemon
  juice

2 teaspoons tahini

¾ teaspoon kosher salt

¾ teaspoon freshly cracked
  black pepper

Drumsticks and Pita

Juice from 1 large lemon (about
  ¼ cup)

¼ cup plus 1 tablespoon extra
  virgin olive oil

4 garlic cloves, minced

2 teaspoons minced fresh
  oregano leaves

2 teaspoons minced fresh dill

¾ teaspoon kosher salt

½ teaspoon freshly cracked
  black pepper

1½ pounds large chicken
  drumsticks (about 5)

4 quality fluffy pita breads (not
  pita pockets)

I BASED THIS HUMMUS ON MY FATHER'S, which he made in his Greek deli for over 30 years. It's intensely garlicky, but in the best possible way, and when it's paired with roasted Mediterranean chicken, you have a truly winning flavor combination. I will say, though, that using good pita makes all the difference here. Do not use the dry pita "pockets" that have holes cut horizontally through the center of the pita, use whole pitas that have not been cut, as these are moist and much fluffier. After making these pita toasts, you'll appreciate that lightly brushing fresh pita with olive oil and toasting it on a griddle is one of life's most simple pleasures. • makes 16 toasts

Preheat the oven to 375°F.

For the hummus, combine the garbanzo beans, olive oil, garlic, lemon juice, tahini, salt, and black pepper in a food processor and blend until completely smooth. Cover and refrigerate.

For the drumsticks, in a large bowl, combine the lemon juice, ¼ cup of the olive oil, the minced garlic, oregano, dill, salt, and black pepper and whisk together. Coat the drumsticks in the olive oil mixture and place on a baking sheet. Bake for 45 to 55 minutes, until the skin becomes golden and crisp and the juices run clear. Let cool slightly before removing the meat from the bones and setting it aside.

For the pita, heat a large skillet over medium heat. Lightly brush both sides of the pita breads with the remaining tablespoon olive oil. Toast one pita in the pan until lightly golden on each side. Remove from the pan and cut the pita into 4 slices. Repeat until all the pita is toasted and quartered.

To assemble, generously spread each pita slice with hummus and top with a piece of the chicken. Serve immediately.

Grilled Dijon Chicken Endives

I LOVE THIS RECIPE BECAUSE OF HOW WONDERFUL these taste, but also because of how easy it is to eat them. Each endive leaf forms a little boat for the filling to rest in, and makes for a perfect passed appetizer at parties. Chicken drumsticks are coated in a honey mustard mixture and roasted until shimmering and juicy. The meat is taken off the bone and paired with apple slices, aged Gouda, fig jam, and flake sea salt inside of each endive leaf, creating a wonderful interplay of flavors and textures. • makes about 18 filled endive leaves

---

¾ cup Dijon mustard

¼ cup extra virgin olive oil

¼ cup honey

¼ cup dry white wine

2 tablespoons light brown sugar

1 teaspoon dried thyme

¾ teaspoon kosher salt

1½ pounds large drumsticks (about 5)

3 Belgian endives

3 tablespoons fig jam

1 ounce aged Gouda, cut into 2-inch-long shavings

1 large apple, cored and cut into ⅛-inch-thick slices

Flake sea salt

Combine the mustard, olive oil, honey, wine, brown sugar, thyme, and salt in the pitcher of a blender and puree until smooth. Transfer ¼ cup of the mixture to a bowl, cover, and set aside in the refrigerator. Pour the remaining mixture into a large resealable plastic bag along with the drumsticks. Press out as much air as possible before sealing. Refrigerate for at least 4 hours or overnight.

In a charcoal grill, heat coals until they're pale grey and glowing orange. Move the hot coals to one side of the grill and place the drumsticks on the grill rack on the opposite (cooler) side, with the meatier end closest to the coals. Grill, covered, turning occasionally, until the drumsticks are cooked through and the juices run clear, 30 to 40 minutes, brushing with the reserved ¼ cup marinade halfway through. Allow to cool before removing the meat from the bones and cutting the meat into roughly 2-inch long and 1-inch wide pieces.

Gently peel the leaves off the endives. Smear ½ teaspoon of the fig jam across an endive leaf. Add a shaving of Gouda, one of the apple slices, and a piece of the chicken and top with a pinch of flake sea salt and drizzle with the reserved sauce. Repeat with the remaining ingredients.

Chicken Nachos *with Arbol Chili Sauce*

Chicken

½ teaspoon kosher salt

¼ teaspoon freshly cracked black pepper

¼ teaspoon ancho chili powder

¼ teaspoon cumin

1 tablespoon extra virgin olive oil

1 large chicken breast (about 1¼ pounds), bone in and skin on

Arbol Chili Sauce

4 dried arbol chiles, stems cut off and seeds emptied and discarded

½ cup extra virgin olive oil

1⅓ cups chicken stock

7 tablespoons tomato paste

1 tablespoon minced fresh oregano leaves

½ teaspoon cumin

½ teaspoon dried ancho chili powder

¼ teaspoon dried chipotle chili powder

Nachos

4 cups tortilla chips

1 cup shredded Mexican blend cheese

1 red bell pepper, sliced

½ cup black beans

1 jalapeño chile, seeded and diced

THESE NACHOS. YOU GUYS. THEY ARE SO, SO GOOD. The homemade arbol chili sauce really makes the nachos shine, and it only takes about 20 minutes, which is super short for such a flavorful sauce. You can find dried arbol chiles in the Mexican food aisle of nearly any major grocery store. They have an earthy, almost smoky aroma and flavor, which complements the chicken perfectly. As you simmer them in the chicken stock, their dried exterior softens and soaks up the flavor of the stock. Then once you puree the sauce and toss it with the nacho fixings, you roast everything in the oven to keep the chips poking out at the top nice and crispy, creating a luscious gooey layer of toppings underneath. • serves 4

Preheat the oven to 350°F.

For the chicken, mix together the salt, black pepper, ancho chili powder, and cumin in a small bowl. Rub the olive oil over the chicken and then coat with the spice mixture. Place on a small baking sheet and roast for 35 to 45 minutes, until the skin is golden and the chicken is cooked through. Remove, leaving the oven on, and let cool. Peel the skin off the chicken and remove the meat from the bone by gently easing your fingers underneath the breast meat to peel it off the bone in one large piece, then pull apart into shreds using two forks. Set aside.

For the arbol chili sauce, in a medium saucepan, cook the dried arbol chiles in the oil over medium-low heat until the chiles soften and the oil turns slightly red, about 5 minutes. Add the stock, tomato paste, oregano, cumin, ancho chili powder, and chipotle chili powder and stir to combine. Simmer until thickened slightly, about 15 minutes. Puree in a blender or food processor until smooth. Set aside.

For the nachos, in a large bowl, pour half of the arbol chili sauce over the chips and toss gently to coat. In a separate bowl, toss together the chicken, ¾ cup of the shredded cheese, the bell pepper, beans, jalapeño, and remaining sauce. Spread half of the chicken mixture in a medium casserole dish. Lay the chips over the chicken mixture and top with the remaining chicken mixture. Sprinkle with the remaining ¼ cup grated cheese. Bake for about 15 minutes, until the cheese is melted and the sauce is bubbling. Serve immediately.

CURRIED CHICKEN SAMOSAS

Dough

2¼ cups all-purpose flour

1 teaspoon onion powder

½ teaspoon caraway seeds

½ teaspoon kosher salt

¼ teaspoon cumin

¼ cup plus 1 tablespoon extra
  virgin olive oil

6 to 9 tablespoons water

Filling

½ pound Yukon gold potatoes

1 tablespoon extra virgin
  olive oil

½ pound boneless skinless
  chicken breast (about 1)

5 garlic cloves, minced

1 tablespoon minced fresh
  ginger

1½ teaspoons curry powder

1½ teaspoons kosher salt

¼ teaspoon caraway

¼ teaspoon turmeric

¼ teaspoon cardamom

2 tablespoons vegetable stock

½ cup shredded spinach

½ teaspoon ground coriander

½ teaspoon cumin

½ teaspoon garam masala

Canola oil, for frying

SAMOSAS ARE A TRADITIONAL INDIAN PASTRY that are usually stuffed with curried potatoes and other vegetables. Here the potatoes and curry remain, but succulent chicken breast meat adds another savory element. Spinach, garlic, and ginger are mashed into the potatoes along with a variety of exotic spices and seasonings, creating a crispy little pocket packed with flavor. • makes 14 samosas

For the dough, in a bowl, mix together the flour, onion powder, caraway seeds, salt, and cumin until combined. Add the olive oil and pinch together with your fingers until the dough forms a sand-like consistency. Add 6 tablespoons of the water, 1 tablespoon at a time, and knead until the dough comes together and forms a smooth dough, about 3 minutes. If it is crumbly and won't come together, add 1 to 3 more tablespoons of water and knead until it becomes smooth and cohesive. Cover and refrigerate for 30 minutes to 4 hours.

For the filling, bring a medium pot of water to a boil with a pinch of salt. Add the potatoes and boil until they're tender when pierced with a fork. Remove them with a slotted spoon and allow them to cool to room temperature before peeling and cutting into roughly 1-inch cubes. Set aside.

Heat the olive oil in a medium frying pan over medium heat. Add the chicken breast and cook, turning occasionally, until browned on both sides and cooked through. Set aside. To the pan, add the garlic, ginger, curry powder, salt, caraway, turmeric, and cardamom and toast, stirring occasionally, for 2 minutes. Add the potatoes, stock, spinach, coriander, cumin, and garam masala and stir to combine. Cook, stirring occasionally, for 4 minutes more while you finely dice the chicken breast meat. Remove the pan from the heat and use a potato masher to crush the mixture so that the potatoes are crumbly but not completely mashed. Stir in the chicken and set aside.

Form the dough into a cylinder and cut into 7 equally thick slices. Lay a kitchen towel over the slices to keep them from drying out while you're working. Roll out one of the slices to a 6-inch round about ⅛ inch thick. Use a sharp knife or pizza cutter to cut the circle in half to form two half moons. Take a half moon, dip your finger in a bowl of water, and run it down the straight line of the half moon. Bring the two ends of the straight line together, forming a cone with its point at the center of the line and the

straight edges slightly overlapping. Pinch the edges together all the way down to the point to create a firm cone.

Place about 1 tablespoon of filling in the cone. Dip your finger in water, run it around half the interior edge of the opening, and press the two sides of the opening together to seal in the filling. Place the samosa on a baking sheet, seam-side down, with the pointed end facing up. Repeat until all the samosas have been assembled.

Add canola oil to a large pot until the oil is at least 4 inches deep and 4 inches away from the top of the pot. Heat to 350°F. Working in batches if necessary, add the samosas and fry until golden brown on all sides, about 3 minutes. Remove using tongs or a slotted spoon and set aside on a wire rack lined with paper towels. Let cool for 20 minutes before serving.

Beet Barbecue Chicken Wings

1 medium beet, peeled and quartered

1 teaspoon extra virgin olive oil

¼ cup honey

¼ cup ketchup

1 tablespoon water

1 tablespoon apple cider vinegar

1 teaspoon soy sauce

1 teaspoon Worcestershire sauce

1 teaspoon chipotle chili powder

2 pounds chicken wings

THE SWEETNESS OF JUST A SINGLE SUGAR BEET makes for the perfect barbecue sauce addition, especially when the beet has been roasted to caramelize the sugars within. The roasted beet is pureed with honey, ketchup, cider vinegar, soy sauce, and other ingredients to create a spicy sweet coating for crispy baked chicken wings. It also makes the most vibrant appetizer ever, with the entirety of the dish striking a lovely magenta hue, pleasing to both the palate and the eye. • serves 4

Preheat the oven to 425°F.

In a bowl, toss the quartered beet with the olive oil. Transfer to a small baking pan and roast for about 20 minutes, until softened slightly but not cooked all the way through. Keep the oven on.

Puree the roasted beet, honey, ketchup, water, vinegar, soy sauce, Worcestershire sauce, and chipotle chili powder in a blender until thick and smooth. Divide the sauce into two equal portions.

In a large bowl, toss the chicken wings with one portion of the sauce to coat. Spread them out in an even layer on a baking sheet, not touching each other, and roast for 35 to 45 minutes, until cooked through and crispy. Remove from the pan with tongs and toss with the second portion of the sauce. Serve immediately.

Honey-Mustard Baked Chicken Wings

THIS IS A NO-FRILLS RECIPE FOR CLASSIC HONEY-MUSTARD wings, and that's because all you really need is mustard, honey, and chicken. They match perfectly: the tangy bite of mustard subdued by sweet honey; the succulent skin of chicken wings absorbing both flavors while crisping up in the oven. I did add smoked paprika, because the only thing that could make these better was a hint of smoke. It plays perfectly off the sweet-and-sour flavors, and adds a little more color to this classic and delicious appetizer. • serves 4

⅔ cup whole grain mustard

½ cup honey

½ teaspoon smoked paprika

½ teaspoon kosher salt

¼ teaspoon mustard powder

2 pounds chicken wings

Preheat the oven to 400°F.

In a large bowl, whisk together the mustard, honey, paprika, salt, and mustard powder until smooth. Add the wings and toss to coat. Transfer the wings to a baking sheet and bake for 35 to 45 minutes, until golden and crisp around the edges.

Chicken Quesadillas *with Slow-Roasted Cherry Tomatoes and Roasted Tomatillo Salsa*

Roasted Tomatillo Salsa

1 pound tomatillos, husks removed

2 jalapeño chiles, cut in half with cap and seeds removed

8 garlic cloves, crushed

1 medium yellow onion, minced

⅓ cup minced fresh cilantro

2 tablespoons freshly squeezed lemon juice

2 teaspoons extra virgin olive oil

¾ teaspoon kosher salt

¼ teaspoon freshly cracked black pepper

Slow-Roasted Cherry Tomatoes

1 pound tomatoes, cut in half

1 tablespoon extra virgin olive oil

1 teaspoon kosher salt

½ teaspoon freshly cracked black pepper

Quesadillas

1 pound boneless skinless chicken breasts (about 2)

½ teaspoon kosher salt, plus extra for seasoning

½ teaspoon freshly cracked black pepper

½ teaspoon ground chipotle pepper powder

3 tablespoons extra virgin olive oil

4 large tortillas

16 ounces queso fresco

THIS RECIPE CALLS FOR MY FAVORITE PRESERVATION METHOD ever —that's slow-roasting cherry tomatoes. I add a roasted tomatillo salsa for dipping the quesadillas, which pretty much makes for the tastiest quesadillas around. I usually roast cherry tomatoes straight from my garden in large batches and freeze the baking sheet with the roasted halved tomatoes on it. I then store the frozen tomatoes in a few mason jars in the freezer, making it easier to grab a few out at a time to use in sandwiches, stews, soups, and my all-time favorite use, quesadillas. • makes 4 quesadillas

For the roasted tomatillo salsa, preheat the oven to 400°F. Place the tomatillos, jalapeños, and garlic on a baking sheet and roast for 15 minutes, until slightly softened. Let cool for 20 minutes before pureeing in a blender or food processor with the onion, cilantro, lemon juice, olive oil, salt, and black pepper. Cover and refrigerate for up to 1 week. (Makes 2 cups salsa.)

For the slow-roasted cherry tomatoes, reduce the oven temperature to 325°F. In a large bowl, toss the tomatoes with the olive oil, salt, and black pepper. Spread out in an even layer on a baking sheet and roast for 1 hour and 15 minutes to 1 hour 25 minutes, until they have shrunk, flattened slightly, wrinkled, and begin to look like sun-dried tomatoes. Set aside.

For the quesadillas, rub the chicken breasts with the salt, black pepper, and chipotle chili powder. Heat the olive oil in a medium frying pan over medium heat. Add the chicken and cook, turning occasionally, until golden on both sides and cooked through, 6 to 8 minutes per side. Once cool enough to handle, cut into ½-inch-thick strips.

To assemble, lay a tortilla flat on a clean work surface. Sprinkle 2 ounces of the queso fresco across half of the tortilla. Add one-fourth of the chicken strips and one-fourth of the roasted cherry tomatoes. Sprinkle another 2 ounces queso fresco over the top and fold the tortilla in half. Repeat with the remaining ingredients.

Sprinkle a pinch of salt in a tortilla pan or large frying pan and heat over medium-high heat. Place a quesadilla on the pan and toast until lightly golden on both sides and the cheese inside is completely melted, about 2 minutes per side. Remove and repeat with the remaining quesadillas. Serve with the roasted tomatillo salsa.

Coconut Chicken Strips
with Mango Dipping Sauce

I'VE ALWAYS BEEN A BIG FAN OF COCONUT, but have never been a huge shrimp person so coconut shrimp was always a bit so-so for me. But then I bypassed the shrimp issue and used chicken breast tenders instead. Paired with a homemade mango dipping sauce, my coconut chicken is everything I love about tropical foods in one insanely delicious appetizer. Seriously, my taste buds basically exploded with happiness when I first tried it. And it's now one of my go-to recipes for parties since it's always a crowd-pleaser and there are never any leftovers (which may or may not be a good thing). • serves 4

For the mango dipping sauce, blend the mango, cream, lime juice, honey, and chili powder in a blender or food processor until smooth. Set aside.

For the coconut chicken, add canola oil to a medium frying pan until the oil is 1 inch deep and heat to 350°F.

While the oil is heating, in a medium bowl, whisk together the flour, salt, and black pepper. Add the wheat beer, honey, and chili garlic sauce and stir until a batter forms. Empty the coconut flakes into a large shallow dish.

Pat the chicken tenders dry with a paper towel, then dip in the batter. Gently shake off any excess batter before dredging the tenders in the coconut flakes to coat. Use tongs to place half the chicken in the frying pan and fry, turning once, until golden brown on each side and completely cooked through, 3 to 4 minutes per side.

Remove and drain on a wire rack lined with paper towels. Repeat with the remaining chicken breast tenders. Garnish with the cilantro. Serve with the mango dipping sauce.

Mango Dipping Sauce

1 large ripe mango, peeled and cut into cubes

3 tablespoons heavy cream

3 tablespoons freshly squeezed lime juice

1 tablespoon honey

¼ teaspoon arbol or red chili powder

Coconut Chicken

Canola oil, for frying

1 cup all-purpose flour

1 teaspoon kosher salt

¼ teaspoon freshly cracked black pepper

¾ cup wheat beer

3 tablespoons honey

1 teaspoon chili garlic sauce

4 cups unsweetened coconut flakes

1 pound chicken breast tenders

1 tablespoon cilantro for garnish

FRIED CHICKEN AND CRAB BASKETS

1 shallot, minced

1 garlic clove, minced

1 tablespoon extra virgin olive oil

½ pound ground chicken

½ teaspoon kosher salt

½ teaspoon freshly cracked black pepper

4 ounces cream cheese, at room temperature

3 ounces drained crab meat

½ teaspoon Old Bay seasoning

1 (12-ounce) package wonton wrappers

Warm water, for assembly

Canola oil, for frying

THIS RECIPE IS BASED ON A CHILDHOOD FAVORITE at the local Chinese restaurant my dad took us to, although I am fairly certain that most Chinese restaurants have a version of this rich fried appetizer called Crab Rangoon. It's essentially crab meat and cream cheese wrapped up in a wonton wrapper and deep-fried, so pretty tasty all around. But then when you add savory ground chicken and Old Bay seasoning, you get a morsel that's packed from top to bottom with a variety of delicious flavors and textures. • makes about 44 baskets

---

Cook the shallot and garlic in the olive oil in a large frying pan over medium heat, stirring occasionally, until softened and slightly translucent, about 5 minutes. Add the ground chicken, salt, and pepper and cook, stirring occasionally, until nearly cooked through, breaking apart the chicken with the end of your spoon. Set aside.

In a medium bowl, mix together the cream cheese, crab meat, and Old Bay until combined.

To assemble, place 1 teaspoon of the chicken mixture and 1 teaspoon of the crab mixture in the center of a wonton wrapper. Dip your finger in the warm water and trace a circle around the edge of the wrapper. Bring the edges up around the filling and pinch together with your fingertips, creating a small parcel. Repeat with the remaining wrappers and filling.

Add canola oil to a large pot until the oil is about 3 inches deep. Heat the oil to 350°F over medium-high heat. In batches, add the baskets and fry, turning as necessary, until golden brown on all sides, about 2 minutes per side As the baskets finish, remove with a slotted spoon and drain on a large plate lined with paper towels. Serve immediately.

Chicken-Stuffed, Bacon-Wrapped Dates
with Gorgonzola

ROSEMARY PERFECTLY ANCHORS CHICKEN to the flavors of dates and bacon here: The herb is sweet enough to go along with the dates, but savory enough to bring out the succulent flavors of the chicken and bacon. And the Gorgonzola does a wonderful job of cutting through the sweet and salty flavors to deliver a strong and creamy zing at the end of each bite. Really, there's not much more you could ask for in an appetizer. • makes about 24 stuffed and wrapped dates

¾ pound chicken drumsticks (about 3)

1 tablespoon extra virgin olive oil

¾ teaspoon kosher salt

¾ teaspoon dried rosemary

½ teaspoon freshly cracked black pepper

24 dates, pitted

3 ounces Gorgonzola cheese

12 strips regular cut bacon, cut crosswise in half

Preheat the oven to 375°F.

Coat the chicken with the olive oil, salt, rosemary, and black pepper and place on a baking sheet. Bake for 45 minutes to 1 hour, until the skin is golden and the chicken is cooked through. Let cool before removing the meat from the bones. Discard the bones. Tear the meat into 24 small pieces.

Cut a date lengthwise down one side and open it up like a book. Place 1 piece of the chicken meat inside with 1 teaspoon of the Gorgonzola cheese. Wrap the stuffed date with a strip of the bacon and place it on a baking sheet. Repeat with the remaining ingredients.

Bake for 20 to 25 minutes, until the bacon is cooked through.

WHOLE & ROASTED

Blood Orange Roast Chicken

Orange Brine and Chicken

8 cups water

¼ cup freshly squeezed orange juice

6 tablespoons kosher salt

1 teaspoon cinnamon

1 whole chicken (about 4 pounds), innards removed

Blood Orange Glaze

¼ cup chicken stock

3 tablespoons blood orange juice

3 tablespoons light brown sugar

2 tablespoons white wine

2 tablespoons rendered duck fat

1 teaspoon kosher salt

¼ teaspoon cinnamon

¼ teaspoon allspice

¼ teaspoon ground cardamom

To Roast the Chicken

1 tablespoon rendered duck fat

2 teaspoons minced fresh rosemary leaves

1 teaspoon kosher salt

1 sprig fresh rosemary

3 blood oranges, cut into twelfths

BLOOD ORANGE SEASON COMES AROUND towards the middle of winter and typically lasts until early spring; when it does, this is the first thing I make with the sweet and almost floral-tasting citrus. They make for the most amazing glaze, particularly when you bring white wine, brown sugar, and duck fat to the mix. You can find rendered duck fat in a little plastic tub at most natural food stores in the frozen meat area. It adds that extra richness that a fruit like blood orange calls for, and makes for an unforgettable roast chicken. You will need to brine the chicken overnight. • serves 4

To brine the chicken, in a large bowl, whisk together the water, orange juice, salt, and cinnamon until combined. Place the chicken in a gallon-size resealable plastic bag and empty the brine into the bag with the chicken. Press out as much air as possible before sealing the bag and refrigerating it. Allow the chicken to rest in the brine overnight.

Preheat the oven to 425°F.

For the glaze, in a small saucepan, bring the stock, blood orange juice, brown sugar, wine, duck fat, salt, cinnamon, allspice, and cardamom to a boil over medium-high heat, stirring occasionally. Reduce the heat to low and simmer until thickened slightly, about 10 minutes. Set aside.

To roast the chicken, remove the chicken from the brine, rinse lightly, and pat dry. Rub it down inside and out with the duck fat, minced rosemary, and salt. Place the chicken in a roasting pan, place the rosemary sprig in the cavity, and truss. Arrange the blood orange slices in the pan around the chicken. Pour the glaze into the pan around the chicken and lightly brush the chicken with the glaze.

Roast for 15 minutes. Reduce the temperature to 375°F and continue roasting, brushing the bird with the pan drippings every 15 minutes, for 50 minutes to 1 hour more, until a thermometer inserted into the thigh of the bird reads at least 165°F.

Allow the bird to rest for 20 minutes before carving and serving.

CHICKEN POMELO SALAD

THE FIRST TIME I HAD POMELO SALAD was in Thailand, and the flavor and presentation stuck with me. Pomelo is a citrus fruit whose interior color ranges from the blushed pink of a grapefruit to the yellow of a ripe lemon. The flavor is similar to grapefruit, but with a slightly sweeter taste. The membrane of the pomelo is especially sturdy so you can actually shred the slices into small strips of juicy fruit, which makes it perfect for tossing into salads like this one. Here the fruity pomelo is paired with chicken, fresh basil, garlic, and a lime dressing for a light and refreshing meal. • serves 4

Preheat the oven to 400°F.

Rub the chicken with the olive oil until well coated. Then rub with the ginger, garlic, salt, and red pepper flakes. Place on a baking sheet and roast for 30 to 40 minutes, until the skin is lightly golden and a thermometer inserted into the breast reads 165°F. Set aside to cool completely. Once cooled, remove the meat from the bone by curving your fingers underneath the breast meat and gently pulling it as a whole. Cut the meat into roughly 1-inch-thick slices and set aside.

Cut one pomelo into quarters and gently separate each wedge of fruity pulp from the rind. Discard the rind and use your fingers to gently pull apart the thread-like pockets of fruit, taking care not to crush them and release their juices. Repeat with the other pomelo.

For the lime dressing, in a bowl, mix together all the ingredients until well blended.

To assemble the salad, toss together the chicken, pomelo, and dressing. Top with the fresh basil and red pepper flakes, if desired.

Chicken

2 pounds chicken breasts, bone in and skin on

2 tablespoons extra virgin olive oil

1 tablespoon grated fresh ginger

2 garlic cloves, minced

2 teaspoons kosher salt

½ teaspoon red pepper flakes

2 large pomelos

2 tablespoons fresh minced basil

½ teaspoon red pepper flakes (optional)

Lime Dressing

1 teaspoon grated lime zest

¼ cup plus 2 tablespoons freshly squeezed lime juice

2 teaspoons fish sauce

2 teaspoons sesame oil

2 teaspoons light brown sugar

2 teaspoons diced fresh ginger

2 garlic cloves, minced

½ teaspoon kosher salt

Roast Chicken Quarters
with Fingerling Potatoes and Garlic

2 tablespoons minced fresh thyme leaves

1½ teaspoons dried savory

1½ teaspoons kosher salt

¾ teaspoon mustard powder

½ teaspoon garlic powder

½ teaspoon paprika

2 pounds fingerling potatoes

1 head garlic, broken up into cloves, unpeeled

3 tablespoons extra virgin olive oil

1½ pounds large chicken leg quarters (about 2), bone in and skin removed

CHICKEN QUARTERS ARE MY FAVORITE PART OF THE BIRD. The connected thighs and drumsticks are one beautiful and succulent cut of meat. Here they're roasted alongside heirloom fingerling potatoes and whole cloves of garlic. The fun thing about keeping the garlic cloves in their papery skin is that the moisture is trapped inside, so you end up with individually roasted cloves of garlic that don't turn dry and crunchy in the oven, but instead transform into tiny pockets of spreadable roasted garlic. I also keep the skins on the fingerling potatoes, since the skin is usually relatively thin on these varieties, and it adds an extra crispness to the exterior of the potatoes. • serves 2

Preheat the oven to 375°F.

In a small bowl, mix together the thyme, savory, salt, mustard powder, garlic powder, and paprika. Toss the potatoes and garlic cloves with half of the spice mixture and 1 tablespoon of the olive oil. Empty into a large casserole dish.

Rub the chicken with the remaining 2 tablespoons olive oil and remaining spice mixture. Arrange in the casserole with the potatoes and garlic around the chicken. Bake for 1 hour to 1 hour 15 minutes, until the potatoes are soft when poked with a fork and the chicken is cooked through. Serve immediately.

LEMON CHICKEN DRUMSTICKS

I DON'T KNOW IF IT HAS TO DO WITH MY GREEK ANCESTRY, but chicken and lemon are one of the most simple and classic pairings in my book. The acidity and freshness of the lemon contrasts beautifully with the richness of the meat, and when you add fresh herbs you get a flavor combination that seems to transport you to a Mediterranean villa. • serves 4

Preheat the oven to 375°F.

In a large bowl, whisk together the lemon juice, olive oil, garlic, crème fraîche, oregano, rosemary, dill, salt, and black pepper. Add the drumsticks and toss to coat. Empty everything into a roasting pan and roast for 45 to 55 minutes, until golden brown on the outside and the juices run clear. Serve immediately.

Juice from 2 large lemons (about ½ cup)

¼ cup extra virgin olive oil

4 garlic cloves, minced

1 tablespoon crème fraîche or sour cream

1 tablespoon minced fresh oregano leaves

1 tablespoon minced fresh rosemary leaves

1 teaspoon minced fresh dill

¾ teaspoon kosher salt

½ teaspoon freshly cracked black pepper

4 large chicken drumsticks (about 1¼ pounds)

Gourmet Beer Can(less) Chicken

Marinade and Chicken

¾ cup pale ale beer

¾ cup chicken stock

2 tablespoons sherry vinegar

1 tablespoon extra virgin olive oil

1 teaspoon dried thyme

1 teaspoon kosher salt

1 whole chicken (4 to 5 pounds), innards removed

To Roast the Chicken

1 cup pale ale beer

2 tablespoons freshly squeezed lemon juice

1½ teaspoons kosher salt

1 teaspoon onion powder

1 teaspoon garlic powder

1 teaspoon minced fresh oregano leaves

½ teaspoon freshly cracked black pepper

¼ teaspoon cumin

2 medium yellow onions, peeled and quartered

2 large lemons, quartered

8 garlic cloves, peeled and cut in half

THERE'S SOMETHING ABOUT THE BUBBLINESS and flavor of beer that makes for a particularly delicious chicken. But rather than stuffing the chicken with an open can of beer, this recipe allows the chicken to both marinate and roast in it, creating an incredibly moist and juicy bird. The chicken is spatchcocked and flattened over fresh onions, lemons, garlic, and spices, creating a seal over the vegetables in the pot that allows all the flavors to bubble up into the flesh of the bird as it cooks, while the skin gets nice and crispy on top, making a gourmet-quality beer-basted bird. • serves 4

To marinate the chicken, in a bowl, stir together the beer, stock, vinegar, olive oil, thyme, and salt. Place the chicken in a large gallon-size resealable plastic bag and add the marinade. Press as much air as possible out of the bag before sealing. Refrigerate for at least 4 hours or overnight.

To roast the chicken, preheat the oven to 375°F.

In a 6-quart round Dutch oven, stir together the beer, lemon juice, salt, onion powder, garlic powder, oregano, pepper, and cumin. Place the onions, lemons, and garlic in the pot and toss to coat.

Remove the chicken from the marinade and place on a clean work surface. Spatchcock the chicken (see page 17), flatten, and place on top of the ingredients in the pot. The flattened chicken should fill the pot from side to side. Spoon some of the liquid in the pot over the bird. Cover and roast for 30 minutes. Increase the oven temperature to 425°F. Uncover the pot and roast, basting every 15 minutes, for 1 hour to 1 hour and 15 minutes, until the chicken is deeply golden and cooked through. Allow the chicken to rest for 20 minutes before carving.

Chicken Quarters *with Parsnip Puree*

There's something almost magical about parsnips roasted with a bit of salt and butter. They turn sweet and taste like caramelized onions, but with the texture of potatoes. Once you puree them, you end up with a mashed potato replacement that tastes better than any mashed spuds you could have ever dreamed of. Serve as a bed for beautifully roasted chicken quarters that have been coated in rosemary, sage, and garlic powder for a stellar dinner. I recommend dipping each forkful of chicken in the pureed parsnips, that way you get the savory crisp skin of the chicken and the creamy caramelized root vegetable in every bite. • serves 2

Preheat the oven to 400°F. Line a baking sheet with foil.

For the chicken, in a small bowl, mix together the rosemary, garlic powder, salt, black pepper, sage, and mustard powder. Rub the chicken with the olive oil and spice mixture until coated. Place in a small roasting pan and add the stock and butter. Roast on the lowest rack for about 1 hour, until the chicken is cooked through and the skin is golden brown.

Meanwhile, for the parsnip puree, in a medium bowl, toss the parsnips with the butter, ½ teaspoon of the salt, and the black pepper until coated. Place the parsnips on the baking sheet and roast on the top rack for 45 minutes to 1 hour, until soft when pierced with a fork.

Place the parsnips in a food processor with the crème fraîche, cream, onion powder, garlic powder, and remaining ½ teaspoon salt; puree until smooth. Serve the parsnip puree alongside the chicken. Garnish with a fresh sprig of rosemary, if desired.

Chicken

2 teaspoons minced fresh rosemary leaves

½ teaspoon garlic powder

½ teaspoon kosher salt

¼ teaspoon freshly cracked black pepper

¼ teaspoon rubbed dried sage

¼ teaspoon mustard powder

2 large chicken leg quarters (about 1½ pounds), bone in and skin on

2 tablespoons extra virgin olive oil

¼ cup chicken stock

2 tablespoons unsalted butter

Parsnip Puree

1 pound parsnips, peeled and cut into 1-inch pieces

¼ cup unsalted butter, melted

1 teaspoon kosher salt

½ teaspoon freshly ground black pepper

⅓ cup crème fraîche or sour cream

¼ cup heavy whipping cream

1 teaspoon onion powder

½ teaspoon garlic powder

2 sprigs fresh rosemary, for garnish (optional)

Cuban Roast Cornish Game Hens

⅔ cup freshly squeezed lime juice

⅔ cup extra virgin olive oil

6 garlic cloves, minced

2 tablespoons minced fresh oregano leaves

1 teaspoon ground cumin

1 teaspoon kosher salt

4 Cornish game hens (about 1 pound each)

1 cup water

½ small yellow onion, cut into 4 wedges

¼ teaspoon freshly cracked black pepper

CORNISH GAME HENS ARE A BREED OF SMALL CHICKENS that are slaughtered at an earlier age than standard broiler varieties, so they're typically much smaller than your average chicken, usually weighing about 1 pound and making them perfect for individual servings. Here, 4 hens are roasted in the same pot along with classic Cuban flavors like garlic, lime juice, olive oil, onion, and cumin. The flavors from the birds and the marinade simmer away with the evaporating liquids, helping to keep the birds nice and moist. Once finished, they make for an incredibly elegant presentation, with a small golden hen laid out on each plate. • serves 4

In a bowl, mix together the lime juice, olive oil, garlic, oregano, cumin, and salt until combined. Pour the marinade into a large resealable plastic bag and add the hens. Press as much air as possible out of the bag before sealing. Refrigerate for at least 4 hours or overnight.

Preheat the oven to 425°F.

Place the hens and their marinade in a large 6¾-quart oval Dutch oven and add the water. Arrange the onion slices around the birds and sprinkle the black pepper over each.

Roast for 20 minutes. Reduce the heat to 375°F and roast for 1 hour 15 minutes to 1 hour 45 minutes longer, until the hens are golden and cooked through. Allow the birds to rest for 20 minutes before removing from the pot and serving.

Roast Chicken Tabbouleh

TABBOULEH IS A MIDDLE EASTERN SALAD of cooked bulgur tossed with fresh herbs, lemon juice, and vegetables. I like to toss cubes of roasted chicken into the mix. When I lived in Los Angeles I often enjoyed a version of this tabbouleh from the Jewish deli down the street; I loved how the bursting juices of the cherry tomatoes paired with the salty succulent chicken and the bright fresh herbs in the most utterly refreshing way. It makes any incredibly hot day much more bearable. • serves 4

Preheat the oven to 375°F.

Coat the chicken with the 1 teaspoon olive oil, the oregano, 1 teaspoon of the salt, and ½ teaspoon of the black pepper and place on a baking sheet. Roast for about 1 hour, until the skin is golden and the chicken is cooked through. Let cool slightly. Peel the skin off the chicken and remove the meat from the bone by gently easing your fingers underneath the breast meat to peel it off the bone in one large piece, then cut into roughly 1-inch cubes. Set aside.

Bring the stock, water, bulgur, lemon zest, and ¼ teaspoon of the remaining salt to a boil in a medium saucepan over medium heat. Cover, reduce the heat to low, and simmer until the bulgur absorbs the liquid, 12 to 15 minutes. Fluff lightly with a fork and set aside.

In a small bowl, whisk together the lemon juice with the remaining ¼ cup olive oil, remaining ½ teaspoon salt, and remaining ¼ teaspoon black pepper. Set the dressing aside.

In a large bowl, toss together the chicken, bulgur, lemon dressing, tomatoes, parsley, mint, green onions, and garlic until evenly dispersed. Serve immediately.

2 pounds large chicken breasts, bone in and skin on

¼ cup plus 1 teaspoon extra virgin olive oil

½ teaspoon dried oregano

1¾ teaspoons kosher salt

¾ teaspoon freshly cracked black pepper

2 cups chicken stock

½ cup water

1⅓ cups bulgur

1 teaspoon finely grated lemon zest

¼ cup freshly squeezed lemon juice

7 ounces cherry tomatoes, halved

1 cup finely chopped fresh parsley

3 tablespoons finely chopped fresh mint

6 green onions, thinly sliced

5 garlic cloves, minced

Roast Chicken and Pork Roulade
with Apples and Brandy

1 teaspoon kosher salt

1 teaspoon dried thyme

½ teaspoon dried rosemary

½ teaspoon dried rubbed sage

½ teaspoon cinnamon

¼ teaspoon ground ginger

¾ pound boneless skinless chicken breast (about 1), finely chopped

1 medium apple, cored, peeled, and finely diced

1 large shallot, finely diced

2 tablespoons extra virgin olive oil

1 (1¼-pound) pork tenderloin

⅔ cup water

¼ cup dry white wine

2 tablespoons brandy

PORK TENDERLOIN, FLATTENED AND STUFFED with a mixture of chopped chicken, apples, shallots, and spices, is roasted with white wine, stock, and brandy to create a delicious mélange of spicy, sweet, and savory flavors. I love serving this for the presentation factor, since the wrapped up tenderloin with the chicken and apples pouring out of each end makes for a beautiful dish, and it smells exactly what all the warmth of fall should smell like. • serves 6

Preheat the oven to 375°F.

In a small bowl, whisk together the salt, thyme, rosemary, sage, cinnamon, and ginger until combined. In a medium bowl, combine half of the spice mixture with the chicken, apple, shallot, and 1 tablespoon of the olive oil and toss until combined. Cover the filling and refrigerate.

Make a lengthwise cut three quarters through the pork down the center of the tenderloin. Unfold it like a book and lay it flat between two sheets of plastic wrap on a clean work surface. Use a meat mallet to hammer the meat and flatten it so that it is roughly 1 inch thick.

Remove the plastic wrap and rub both sides of the tenderloin with the remaining 1 tablespoon olive oil and remaining spice mixture. Lay it flat and place half of the filling in a straight line lengthwise down the center of the tenderloin.

Roll the tenderloin around the filling, jelly roll-style, until the two sides overlap slightly. Keeping the seam on the side, tie up the tenderloin with kitchen string at 2-inch intervals. Place the remaining filling in a small roasting pan and transfer the tenderloin to the pan, seam facing down. Add the water, wine, and brandy to the pan. Roast for 1 hour to 1 hour 15 minutes, until the internal temperature of the filling reaches 165°F. Let cool for 15 minutes before slicing and serving.

Bacon and Maple Roast Chicken

Maple Marinade and Chicken

¼ cup chicken stock

3 tablespoons pure maple syrup

2 tablespoons white vinegar

2 tablespoons extra virgin olive oil

1 tablespoon kosher salt

1 teaspoon minced fresh thyme leaves

1 whole chicken (about 4 pounds), innards removed

To Roast the Chicken

2 tablespoons pure maple syrup

2 tablespoons pure maple sugar

1½ teaspoons kosher salt

1½ teaspoons dried rosemary

½ teaspoon freshly cracked black pepper

4 strips thick-cut bacon

1 large sweet onion, diced

2 tablespoons extra virgin olive oil

Chicken stock

10 large sprigs fresh rosemary

I JUST MAY HAVE STUFFED STRIPS OF BACON under the skin of the chicken for this one. This is wonderful in two ways (well, it's wonderful in a variety of ways, but for brevity's sake I'm just going to focus on two): First, the chicken skin gets nice and crispy while roasting, but instead of only tasting like chicken skin, it also tastes like bacon. And second, since the bacon is under the skin, its flavors are relatively trapped under there and so, with nowhere else for the bacon juices to go, they start to seep into the breast meat of the bird, turning a relatively moderately flavored cut of meat into a delightfully bacon-filled fillet. Oh, and I also marinated the bird in maple beforehand. Mmmmmmm. • serves 4

To marinate the chicken, whisk together the stock, maple syrup, vinegar, olive oil, salt, and thyme until combined. Coat the chicken inside out with the mixture and place in a resealable gallon-size plastic bag, emptying any excess marinade into the bag. Press out as much air as possible before sealing. Refrigerate overnight or for at least 4 hours.

To roast the chicken, preheat the oven to 350°F.

Remove the chicken from the bag, rinse off any excess marinade, and pat dry with paper towels. Rub the bird down with 1 tablespoon of the maple syrup, inside and out, getting under the skin of the chicken breast while taking care not to tear the skin. (To do so, gently lift the skin off the breast with one hand and with a small paring knife in the other hand, carefully cut through the fat membrane that runs down the center of the chicken breast, taking care not to puncture the skin. Once the membrane has been cut, you should be able to place your hand under the skin of the entire front of the chicken, rather than one side or the other.)

In a small bowl, whisk together the maple sugar, 1 teaspoon of the salt, ¾ teaspoon of the rosemary, and the black pepper. Coat the chicken inside and out with the spice mixture.

Cut 2 of the bacon slices in half. Wedge them flat under the breast skin of the bird, so the four strips of bacon lie side by side under the breast skin.

Dice the remaining 2 strips of bacon. In a bowl, toss together the diced bacon, onion, olive oil, remaining 1 tablespoon maple syrup, remaining ¾ teaspoon rosemary, and remaining ½ teaspoon salt until combined. Empty the mixture into a small roasting pan and pat down to create a bed. Pour stock into the pan until it is ½ inch deep.

Place the chicken in the pan, breast facing up. Place 2 large sprigs of the rosemary in the cavity of the bird and place the remaining 8 in the pan around the chicken. Truss the bird. Tent the entire pan with tinfoil, making sure none of it touches the skin.

Roast, rotating the pan once to ensure even cooking, for about 1 hour and 15 minutes, until the internal temperature of a thigh reaches 165°F. Remove the tinfoil tent for the last 20 minutes of cooking to allow the skin to brown slightly.

Allow the chicken to rest for 20 minutes before carving and serving.

Pear and Vanilla Bean–Brown Butter Roast Chicken

An ode to roast chicken, this recipe has a short list of ingredients, but that's because the ingredients themselves are so delicious that you really want to let their flavors shine through. The chicken is brined the night before to ensure it stays juicy throughout the cooking process, and is then coated in vanilla- and allspice-infused brown butter and stuffed with half a pear. It rests on a bed of onion and pears and roasts away in the oven, allowing the juices from all the fruits to infuse into the bird along with the vanilla. The result is a roast chicken unlike any other: aromatic, juicy, savory, and sweet. It will warm you deep into your bones. • serves 4

To brine the chicken, in a bowl, mix together the water, salt, vanilla extract, and thyme. Place the chicken in a large gallon-size resealable plastic bag and add the brine until nearly full. Press as much air out of the bag as possible and seal. Refrigerate overnight.

For the vanilla bean–brown butter, melt the butter in a small saucepan over medium heat, stirring occasionally. Continue cooking the butter, stirring several times to ensure it cooks evenly, until it turns golden brown and smells toasty. Remove from the heat and use a blunt butter knife to scrape the inside of the vanilla bean pods over the pot, allowing the small vanilla beans to fall into the brown butter. After scraping, add the vanilla pods, vinegar, salt, and allspice to the pot and whisk. Set aside and infuse for 15 minutes.

To roast the chicken, preheat the oven to 425°F.

Evenly distribute the diced onion in a small roasting pan. Remove the chicken from the brine, rinse gently, and pat dry. Place the bird in the pan and rub with half of the brown butter mixture, inside and out, getting under the skin of the breast. Stuff with 2 of the pear quarters. Remove the whole vanilla bean pods from the pot and place inside the chicken as well. Truss the bird. Arrange the remaining pear quarters around the bird and drizzle the remaining brown butter mixture and the stock over the pears and chicken.

Roast for 30 minutes. Reduce the heat to 375°F and roast, turning halfway through, for 1 hour 15 minutes to 1 hour 45 minutes longer, until a thermometer inserted into a thigh of the bird reads at least 165°F. Allow the chicken to rest for 20 minutes before carving.

Vanilla-Thyme Brine and Chicken

8 cups water

6 tablespoons kosher salt

1 teaspoon vanilla extract

1 teaspoon dried thyme

1 large whole chicken (about 5 pounds), innards removed

Vanilla Bean–Brown Butter

8 tablespoons (1 stick) unsalted butter

1 vanilla bean, split in half

1 teaspoon sherry vinegar

1 teaspoon kosher salt

¼ teaspoon allspice

To Roast the Chicken

1 large sweet onion, diced

2 Bosc pears, quartered and cored

1 cup chicken stock

Roast Chicken and Bulgur Salad
with Tangerines and Pomegranate

Roast Chicken

1¾ pounds chicken drumsticks (about 6 large)

2 tablespoons extra virgin olive oil

½ teaspoon kosher salt

½ teaspoon dried ground ginger

¼ teaspoon cinnamon

¼ teaspoon onion powder

Bulgur Salad

1⅓ cups bulgur

2 cups water

¾ cup chicken stock

½ teaspoon ground ginger

¼ teaspoon cinnamon

¼ teaspoon kosher salt

4 tangerines, cut into sixths

⅓ cup pomegranate seeds

1 tablespoon minced fresh mint

2 teaspoons minced fresh dill

Lemon Dressing

¼ cup freshly squeezed lemon juice

2 tablespoons heavy whipping cream

1 tablespoon extra virgin olive oil

½ teaspoon kosher salt

¼ teaspoon allspice

THIS SALAD TAKES ADVANTAGE OF THE TASTY FRUIT available during the winter months. Pomegranates and tangerines tend to come into the markets around December and January, right around the time that I can't stop craving roast chicken. When you combine these three with bulgur made from chicken stock, you end up with a savory and sweet salad that not only tastes incredible but makes for a stunning presentation. • serves 4

To roast the chicken, preheat the oven to 375°F.

Toss the drumsticks with the olive oil, salt, ginger, cinnamon, and onion powder until coated. Spread out on a baking sheet and roast for about 40 minutes, until the skin is golden and crisp and the meat is cooked through and the juices run clear. Let cool before removing the meat from the bones.

For the bulgur salad, bring the bulgur, water, stock, ginger, cinnamon, and salt to a boil in a medium saucepan over medium heat. Cover, reduce the heat to low, and simmer until the bulgur absorbs the liquid, 12 to 15 minutes. Fluff lightly with a fork and transfer to a casserole dish.

Meanwhile, for the lemon dressing, in a bowl, whisk together the lemon juice, cream, olive oil, salt, and allspice until smooth.

Drizzle the dressing over the bulgur and add the chicken, tangerines, pomegranate, mint, and dill and toss until evenly distributed. Serve immediately.

MEDITERRANEAN STUFFED TOMATOES

MY MOTHER HAS BEEN MAKING THESE STUFFED TOMATOES for longer than I can remember. They combine the tang and subtle sweetness of roasted tomatoes with warm and toasty spices like cinnamon, allspice, and nutmeg. Raisins add a spot of sweetness, and fresh mint and oregano contribute a perfectly refreshing flavor. Everything is tossed together with ground chicken, tomato bits, and rice and then stuffed into large heirloom tomatoes. The caps are placed back on and they're roasted until wrinkled and soft and all the flavors have melded together, making for a very healthy dish that doesn't sacrifice flavor. • serves 6

Preheat the oven to 425°F.

Cut the top ½ inch off 6 of the tomatoes and set the caps aside. Use a metal spoon to gently scoop the seedy pulp out of the tomatoes, reserving the pulp and maintaining the structure of the outer wall and bottom of each tomato. Place the hollowed out tomatoes in a roughly 10 by 14-inch casserole. Dice the single remaining tomato and add it to the tomato pulp.

Heat the olive oil in a large pan over medium heat. Add the onion and garlic and cook, stirring occasionally, until softened slightly and fragrant, about 4 minutes. Add the ground chicken and tomato pulp mixture and continue cooking, breaking apart the pieces of chicken with the end of your stirring spoon, until the chicken is nearly cooked through, about 7 minutes. Add the rice, 1 cup of the stock, the raisins, tomato paste, cinnamon, salt, black pepper, allspice, and nutmeg and stir until combined. Simmer, uncovered and stirring every 2 minutes, for 10 minutes, until the rice absorbs some of the liquid. Stir in the mint and oregano and remove the stuffing from the heat.

Gently spoon the stuffing into the tomatoes, taking care not to overstuff them or they will split during cooking. Place the caps on the tops, place the tomatoes in the pan, and spoon any leftover stuffing around them. Pour the remaining 1 cup stock into the pan around the tomatoes. Roast for 40 to 45 minutes, until the tomatoes have softened and the rice is cooked through. Let cool for 15 minutes before serving.

7 large tomatoes

2 tablespoons extra virgin olive oil

1 medium yellow onion, diced

5 garlic cloves, minced

1 pound ground chicken

1 cup uncooked white rice

2 cups chicken stock

¼ cup raisins

2 tablespoons tomato paste

½ teaspoon cinnamon

½ teaspoon kosher salt

½ teaspoon freshly cracked black pepper

¼ teaspoon allspice

¼ teaspoon nutmeg

3 tablespoons minced fresh mint leaves

2 tablespoons minced fresh oregano leaves

Chicken, Pistachio, and Caramelized Fennel Salad

3 teaspoons kosher salt

1½ teaspoons freshly cracked black pepper

1 teaspoon onion powder

1¾ pounds chicken thighs (about 4), bone in and skin on

2 tablespoons extra virgin olive oil

2 tablespoons unsalted butter

6 large fennel bulbs, fronds removed, cut into ½-inch-thick slices

2 shallots, finely diced

6 ounces goat cheese, crumbled

¼ cup chopped shelled roasted pistachios

1 tablespoon minced fresh dill

2 teaspoons freshly squeezed lemon juice

I HAD CARAMELIZED FENNEL BULB FOR THE FIRST TIME at one of my photography workshops when my friend Carey made it for the group. It was pretty much love at first bite; the anise-like flavor of the fennel bulb becomes very muted and a semi-sweet caramelized flavor fills in its place. Toss in some shallots, goat cheese, pistachios, and rich dark meat chicken and you have yourself the most savory salad of them all. • serves 4

Preheat the oven to 450°F.

In a small bowl, mix together 2 teaspoons of the salt, ¾ teaspoon of the black pepper, and the onion powder. Coat the chicken with the olive oil and spice mixture and place on a baking sheet. Roast for about 20 minutes, until the skin is golden and the internal temperature reaches 165°F. Set aside to cool completely.

Once cooled, remove the chicken thigh meat from half of the chicken thighs by reaching underneath the thigh meat and gently but firmly pulling it off the bone. Cut the removed meat into roughly 1-inch-thick strips and set aside.

Melt the butter in a large shallow Dutch oven over medium heat. Add about half of the sliced fennel to the pan in a flat even layer and arrange half of the diced shallots around the fennel. Cook, stirring occasionally, until the fennel is golden on each side and softened, 8 to 10 minutes per side. Transfer the fennel and shallots to a large bowl. Repeat with the remaining fennel and shallots.

Sprinkle the caramelized fennel and shallots with the remaining teaspoon salt and ¾ teaspoon black pepper. To the caramelized fennel, add the chicken strips, goat cheese, pistachios, dill, and lemon juice and toss. Place the remaining whole chicken thighs on top and serve immediately.

GRILLED & FRIED

Brick Chicken

1 teaspoon kosher salt

¾ teaspoon garlic powder

½ teaspoon smoked paprika

½ teaspoon ground cayenne pepper

½ teaspoon ground dried oregano

¼ teaspoon allspice

1 whole chicken (about 4 pounds), innards removed

2 long skewers

1 tablespoon extra virgin olive oil

1 brick, wrapped in tinfoil

½ lemon

An entire spatchcocked chicken is grilled over hot coals with a brick on top of it in this eye-catching dish. The brick heats up on the grill and helps cook the chicken from both sides, allowing the bird to stay juicier by shortening the overall cooking time. I love this cooking method because it not only makes for an incredibly moist grilled chicken, but you can have a lot of fun with the presentation. You can rest the finished bird on a brick, or serve it with the brick placed on top; either way will definitely catch everyone's attention and offer a bit of insight into how the chicken was cooked. • serves 4

Preheat the charcoal grill by heating the coals until they're pale grey and glowing orange, about 20 minutes.

In a small bowl, mix together the salt, garlic powder, paprika, cayenne, oregano, and allspice. Set aside.

Spatchcock the chicken on a clean flat work surface (see page 17), then lay the chicken flat with the skin facing up. Push two long skewers through the chicken to form an X-shape, inserting each into a leg quarter and exiting through the opposite upper corner of the breast. (This will make the bird easier to flip and handle with tongs while you're grilling it, otherwise the spatchcocked chicken will get a bit unruly.)

Rub the chicken down with the olive oil and spice mixture and set aside.

Move the hot coals to one side of the grill and place the chicken, skin side down, on the opposite side of the grill. Place the foil-wrapped brick on top of the chicken and close the lid of the grill, ensuring the vents of the grill are open. Cook until the bird's skin is golden and lightly charred around the edges and the meat is cooked through, 1 hour to 1 hour 15 minutes, turning once if necessary.

Squeeze the lemon half over the chicken and serve immediately.

GRILLED CHICKEN–CAESAR SALAD

NOTHING IS QUITE SO SATISFYING on a hot summer's day as a grilled chicken–Caesar salad. Smoky chicken cuts through a creamy tangy dressing, and radishes and curly frisée add a refreshing crispness. I love using frisée in salads because the long and twisting fronds of the green make many nooks and crannies for the dressing to get caught up in. I like to use heirloom watermelon radishes here, but any radish variety will do. Just note that the older the radish, the more intense the heat, so if you want to err on the milder side, get them from a farmers' market where you can be certain they weren't harvested late. • serves 4

For the dressing, in a blender or food processor, mix together the garlic, lemon juice, anchovy paste, mustard powder, Worcestershire sauce, salt, and pepper. Add the egg and blend until combined. While the blender is running at medium speed, add the olive oil through the small opening in the top of the blender in a steady stream. Blend until thickened and combined then refrigerate for up to 4 days.

For the chicken salad, heat a gas grill to medium heat or heat a grill pan over medium high heat on the stovetop. Coat the chicken breasts with the olive oil, salt, and pepper. Grease the grill grate or grill pan well. Grill the chicken over medium heat until cooked through and deep golden char marks appear on both sides. Let cool before cutting into 1-inch-thick strips.

Toss the chicken with the frisée, radish, croutons, and Parmesan. Top with the desired amount of dressing and serve immediately.

Caesar Dressing

- 3 garlic cloves, peeled
- 2 tablespoons freshly squeezed lemon juice
- 2 teaspoons anchovy paste
- 1 teaspoon mustard powder
- ½ teaspoon Worcestershire sauce
- ½ teaspoon kosher salt
- ½ teaspoon freshly cracked black pepper
- 1 large egg
- ⅓ cup extra virgin olive oil

Chicken Salad

- 1 pound large boneless skinless chicken breasts (about 2)
- 1 tablespoon olive oil
- ¾ teaspoon kosher salt
- ¼ teaspoon freshly cracked black pepper
- 4 cups frisée or other leafy green
- 1 radish, thinly sliced
- ⅔ cup croutons
- ¼ cup freshly grated Parmesan cheese

GRILLED CHICKEN AND ASPARAGUS

SOMETIMES THE SIMPLEST PREPARATIONS ARE THE BEST ONES, and this definitely applies to this pair. Butter, thyme, and a pinch of seasonings are all that season these leg quarters and asparagus before being grilled. The asparagus crisps up slightly at the tips while the interior softens, and the chicken develops a deep golden skin while staying rich and succulent, making the perfect lazy day meal. • serves 2

4 tablespoons unsalted butter

1 tablespoon fresh thyme leaves

1 teaspoon kosher salt

¾ teaspoon freshly cracked black pepper

½ teaspoon garlic powder

½ teaspoon onion powder

2 chicken leg quarters (about 1½ pounds), bone in and skin on

Wooden skewers, soaked in water

1 pound asparagus

Melt the butter in a small frying pan over medium-low heat. Add the thyme and remove from the heat. Allow the thyme to infuse in the butter for 20 minutes before straining them out. Reserve the melted butter.

Preheat the charcoal grill by heating the coals until they're pale grey and glowing orange, about 20 minutes.

In a small bowl, stir together the salt, black pepper, garlic powder, and onion powder. Divide into two equal parts and set aside.

Drizzle a tablespoon of the melted butter mixture over the chicken leg quarters and rub it in to coat. Sprinkle the chicken with half of the spice mixture.

Move the hot coals to one side of the grill and place the chicken leg quarters on the opposite side. Grill until the skin is crispy and the chicken is cooked through, 1 hour to 1 hour 15 minutes, turning 4 times. Set aside.

Skewer the asparagus crosswise with two long skewers so that there's one skewer going through the top ends of all the asparagus and one skewer going through the bottom ends, creating a sheet of asparagus. Brush on both sides with the butter and sprinkle with the remaining spice mixture. Grill over indirect heat until they have turned a vibrant green and wrinkled slightly, 15 to 25 minutes. Serve alongside the chicken.

Chicken and Fruit Couscous Salad
with Lemony Yogurt Dressing

1¼ cups vegetable stock

1 cup couscous

2 tablespoons plus 2 teaspoons extra virgin olive oil

1½ pounds chicken leg quarters (about 2), bone in and skin on

1½ teaspoons kosher salt

½ teaspoon dried rosemary

¼ cup plus 1 tablespoon freshly squeezed lemon juice

2 tablespoons plain full-fat Greek yogurt

1 tablespoon granulated sugar

⅛ teaspoon orange blossom water

⅛ teaspoon vanilla extract

1 cup ripe blackberries

1 large yellow peach, cut into eighths

1 tablespoon fresh basil leaves, for garnish (optional)

THIS FRESH SUMMER SALAD takes advantage of the fruits of the season, and tosses blackberries and peaches in a delicious lemon vinaigrette along with savory couscous and grilled chicken. The lemon provides a lightly sour element that cuts through the sweetness of the fruit, while intensifying the savory qualities of the grilled chicken, creating a delicious meal that's as full of flavor as it is beauty. • serves 4

Preheat the charcoal grill by heating the coals until they're pale grey and glowing orange, about 20 minutes.

Bring the stock to a boil in a small saucepan. Remove from the heat, stir in the couscous and 2 tablespoons of the olive oil, and cover. Rest until all the liquid has been absorbed by the couscous, 5 to 10 minutes. Fluff lightly with a fork and set aside to cool.

Coat the chicken with the remaining 2 teaspoons olive oil, then rub with ½ teaspoon of the salt and the dried rosemary. Move the hot coals to one side of the grill and place the chicken skin side down on the opposite side of the grill. Cook until the skin crisps up and turns golden and the meat is cooked through, about 1 hour, turning 3 to 4 times. Remove from the grill and let cool before removing the meat from the bones and cutting into roughly 1-inch pieces.

In a small bowl, whisk together the lemon juice, yogurt, sugar, orange blossom water, vanilla extract, and remaining 1 teaspoon salt until smooth. In a large bowl, toss together the couscous, chicken, blackberries, and peach slices with the lemon vinaigrette until combined. Garnish with fresh basil leaves, if desired. Serve immediately.

GRILLED SPICED CHICKEN

LAYERS OF SEASONINGS ARE WHAT MAKE THIS CHICKEN so memorable and unique. All the flavors build upon each other and create a charred coating on the chicken while it grills, sealing the juices and flavors inside while it cooks to perfection. I like serving the chicken alongside freshly sliced cucumbers sprinkled with a pinch of sea salt for a cool contrast to the heat of the dish, but it tastes just as wonderful on its own. • serves 4

To marinate the chicken, in a small bowl mix together the lemon juice, olive oil, garlic, ginger, curry powder, and salt until combined. Spatchcock the chicken (see page 17) and then cut in half down the breast with poultry shears. Lay the chicken flat with the skin facing up. Push one long skewer through each chicken half, inserting into a leg quarter and exiting through the upper breast. (This will make the bird easier to flip and handle with tongs while you're grilling it, otherwise the spatchcocked chicken will get a bit unruly.) Place the chicken and the marinade in a large resealable plastic bag, pressing as much air out of the bag as possible before sealing. Refrigerate for at least 4 hours or overnight.

Preheat the charcoal grill by heating the coals until they're pale grey and glowing orange, about 20 minutes.

For the spice mix, in a small bowl, mix together the curry powder, cinnamon, salt, caraway, turmeric, coriander, cumin, black pepper, cardamom, cloves, allspice, and cayenne pepper until combined.

Remove the chicken from the marinade, rinse it, and pat it dry. Rub it down with the olive oil and coat with the spice mixture.

Move the hot coals to one side of the grill and place the chicken on the opposite side. Grill until the skin is crispy and the chicken is cooked through, 1 hour 15 minutes to 1 hour 35 minutes, turning 4 times. Serve.

Lemon Marinade and Chicken

3 tablespoons freshly squeezed lemon juice

3 tablespoons extra virgin olive oil

4 garlic cloves, minced

1 tablespoon grated fresh ginger

1 teaspoon curry powder

1 teaspoon kosher salt

1 small chicken (about 3 pounds), innards removed

Spice Mix

1 tablespoon curry powder

2 teaspoons cinnamon

1½ teaspoons kosher salt

1 teaspoon ground caraway

1 teaspoon turmeric

1 teaspoon coriander

1 teaspoon cumin

1 teaspoon freshly cracked black pepper

¾ teaspoon cardamom

½ teaspoon cloves

½ teaspoon allspice

¼ teaspoon ground cayenne pepper

1 tablespoon extra virgin olive oil

2 long skewers

Greek–Grilled Chicken Salad

1 pound chicken thighs (about 2), bone in and skin on

2 tablespoons plus 1 teaspoon extra virgin olive oil

½ teaspoon ground dried oregano

1 teaspoon kosher salt

¾ teaspoon freshly cracked black pepper

1 tablespoon white vinegar

1 teaspoon freshly squeezed lemon juice

1½ pounds tomatoes, cut into sixths

1 large cucumber, peeled and cut in half lengthwise, then cut in ½-inch-thick slices

½ red onion, coarsely chopped

3 ounces feta cheese stored in brine, drained

3 ounces kalamata olives

1 tablespoon finely chopped fresh oregano leaves

GREEK SALADS ARE TRADITIONALLY CHUNKY and full of large, roughly cut pieces of ripe fruits and vegetables. In this chicken iteration, the addition of feta cheese makes for a nice creamy texture and adds a tart bite, and grilled chicken adds a crisp and juicy texture and infuses deep succulent and smoky flavor throughout the salad. • serves 4

Preheat the charcoal grill by heating the coals until they're pale grey and glowing orange, about 20 minutes.

Coat the chicken in 1 teaspoon of the olive oil, then coat with the dried oregano, ½ teaspoon of the salt, and ¼ teaspoon of the black pepper.

Move the hot coals to one side of the grill and place the chicken, skin side down, on the opposite side of the grill. Grill until the chicken's skin is golden and the meat is cooked through, 50 minutes to 1 hour, turning once. Let cool, then remove the meat from the bones and cut it into roughly 1-inch cubes. Set aside.

In a small bowl, whisk together the vinegar, lemon juice, remaining 2 tablespoons olive oil, remaining ½ teaspoon salt, and remaining ½ teaspoon black pepper. Toss the olive oil mixture with the chicken, tomatoes, cucumber, onion, feta, olives, and fresh oregano until combined. Serve immediately.

Tandoori Chicken

Traditional tandoori chicken is chicken that is coated in a seasoned yogurt sauce and cooked in a large cylindrical clay oven that's heated by coals or burning logs. Here it is grilled on a standard charcoal grill, but the richly spiced yogurt sauce stays close to the traditional preparation. The chicken is marinated for several hours or overnight in a portion of the sauce, then grilled until the skin becomes wonderfully crispy. While the breasts and thighs are finishing, the remaining yogurt sauce is simmered with a dash of tomato paste, creating a warm and rich sauce to drizzle over the chicken right before serving. • serves 4

In a medium bowl, mix together the yogurt, lemon juice, garlic, ginger, cumin, onion powder, salt, coriander, garam masala, cayenne, paprika, cardamom, curry powder, and cloves until combined.

Prick the chicken breasts and thighs all over with a fork and place in a large resealable plastic bag. Add three-fourths of the yogurt sauce and press as much air out of the bag as possible before sealing it. Refrigerate for at least 4 hours or overnight. Cover and refrigerate the remaining yogurt sauce separately.

In a charcoal grill, heat coals until they're pale grey and glowing orange, about 20 minutes. Move the hot coals to one side of the grill and place the chicken breasts and thighs on the opposite side of the grill. Grill until the chicken is cooked through and juices run clear, 1 hour to 1 hour 30 minutes, turning 4 times.

While the chicken is grilling, in a small pot, mix the reserved yogurt sauce, water, and tomato paste together over low heat. Bring the mixture to a simmer and cook for 5 minutes. Brush the finished chicken with the yogurt sauce and serve.

1 cup plain full-fat yogurt

⅓ cup freshly squeezed lemon juice

4 garlic cloves, minced

1 tablespoon grated fresh ginger

1 tablespoon cumin

1 teaspoon onion powder

1 teaspoon kosher salt

1 teaspoon ground coriander

¾ teaspoon garam masala

½ teaspoon ground cayenne pepper

½ teaspoon paprika

½ teaspoon cardamom

¼ teaspoon curry powder

¼ teaspoon cloves

2 chicken breasts (about 2 pounds), bone in and skin on

2 chicken thighs (about 1 pound), bone in and skin on

2 tablespoons water

1 tablespoon tomato paste

GRILLED SPATCHCOCKED CHICKEN
in Plum Sauce

1 small chicken (2 to 3 pounds), innards removed

3 ripe plums, pitted and quartered

½ large yellow onion, chopped

¼ cup soy sauce

¼ cup honey

3 tablespoons rice vinegar

2 tablespoons sesame oil

2 tablespoons light brown sugar

1 teaspoon grated fresh ginger

2 long skewers

THERE'S SOMETHING ABOUT THE SWEET JUICY FLAVOR of a ripe plum that goes perfectly with a sumptuous grilled piece of chicken. In this recipe I make a savory and sweet Asian-inspired plum sauce and use a portion of it as a marinade, then the rest is brushed over the chicken several times during the grilling process to keep the meat moist and the flavor deep. Spatchcocking allows the bird to cook more evenly and in a shorter time on the grill, keeping the meat nice and juicy. Ginger, soy sauce, honey, and sesame oil are just a few of the flavors that seep into the chicken in the process. • serves 4

Spatchcock the chicken (see page 17) and place in a large resealable plastic bag.

Combine the plums, onion, soy sauce, honey, vinegar, sesame oil, brown sugar, and ginger in the pitcher of a blender and puree until smooth. Take ⅓ cup of the plum sauce, cover, and set aside in the refrigerator.

Empty the rest of the plum sauce into the plastic bag with the chicken and press as much air as possible out of the bag before sealing it and placing it in the refrigerator. Refrigerate for at least 4 hours or overnight.

In a charcoal grill, heat coals until they're pale grey and glowing orange, about 20 minutes. Move the hot coals to one side of the grill.

Shake the excess marinade off the chicken. On a flat clean work surface, lay the chicken flat with the skin facing up. Push two long skewers through the chicken so that they form an X-shape, inserting each into a leg quarter and exiting through the opposite upper corner of the breast. This will make the bird easier to flip and handle with tongs while you're grilling it (otherwise the spatchcocked chicken will get a bit unruly).

Place the chicken on the opposite side of the grill from the coals. Grill until the chicken is cooked through and juices run clear, 1 hour 15 minutes to 1 hour 45 minutes, turning 4 times and brushing the chicken with the reserved plum sauce about every 20 minutes. Serve immediately.

Tennessee Hot Chicken
with Quick Dill Pickles

I FIRST HEARD OF TENNESSEE HOT CHICKEN from a South Carolinian I met on a freelance resort photo shoot in the Virgin Islands; she raved about the flavor combinations and I knew I had to give it a try. The cool juicy crunch of the pickles helps soothe the heat from the rich and spicy fried chicken, while the white bread provides a neutral and fluffy bed for all the mains to rest on, slowly absorbing drops and crumbs from the rest of the dish and creating a soft mass of irresistible flavor. • serves 4

For the pickles, bring the vinegar, sugar, salt, peppercorns, and caraway seeds to a boil in a small pot over medium-high heat. Boil rapidly for 1 minute. Pour the mixture over the cucumber in a wide shallow dish. Toss with the fresh dill and steep until cooled to room temperature. Cover and refrigerate for up to 5 days.

For the chicken, heat the olive oil and dried chiles in a medium shallow frying pan over medium-low heat. Simmer until the oil deepens in color, 10 to 15 minutes. Remove from the heat, whisk in 1 tablespoon of the brown sugar, and set aside.

In a medium bowl, whisk together the flour, salt, and remaining tablespoon brown sugar. Set aside. In a separate medium bowl, whisk together the milk, yogurt, eggs, vinegar, cayenne, paprika, and ancho chili until smooth.

Add canola oil to a deep pot so that it is at least 4 inches deep but at least 4 inches from the top of the pot. Heat the oil to 350°F over medium heat. Dredge the chicken in the flour mixture and shake off the excess. Dip it in the batter and let the excess drip off before dredging it in the flour mixture one more time.

Place the chicken in the hot oil, one piece at a time, working in batches as necessary, and fry until golden and cooked through, about 15 minutes. Note that the oil temperature will drop to about 325°F when you add the chicken; keep it at 325°F throughout the frying process and bring it back up to 350°F when you've removed the finished chicken and before you add the next batch. Set the finished chicken aside on a plate lined with paper towels.

Brush the finished chicken with the pepper-steeped oil and serve on top of a bed of the French bread with the quick dill pickles.

Quick Dill Pickles

⅔ cup apple cider vinegar

1½ teaspoons granulated sugar

1 teaspoon kosher salt

6 black peppercorns

¼ teaspoon caraway seeds

1 large (12-ounce) cucumber, thinly sliced

½ teaspoon minced fresh dill

Tennessee Hot Chicken

¼ cup extra virgin olive oil

2 large dried New Mexico chiles, caps and seeds removed

2 tablespoons light brown sugar

3 cups all-purpose flour

1 tablespoon kosher salt

1 cup whole milk

1 cup full-fat plain Greek yogurt

4 large eggs

3 tablespoons apple cider vinegar

2 teaspoons ground cayenne pepper

1 teaspoon smoked paprika

1 teaspoon ancho chili powder

Canola oil, for frying

1 whole chicken (about 4 pounds), cut into parts

4 slices French bread, lightly toasted

Chicken Yakisoba

10 ounces dry soba noodles

4 tablespoons sesame oil

5 tablespoons soy sauce

1 tablespoon plus 2 teaspoons ponzu

2 teaspoons mirin

1 teaspoon grated fresh ginger

½ teaspoon red pepper flakes

3 tablespoons canola oil

5 garlic cloves, minced

2 shallots, diced

1 pound large boneless skinless chicken breasts, cut into 1-inch cubes

1 carrot, peeled and diced

¼ head cabbage, chopped

In Japanese *yaki* means grill and *soba* refers the thick style of egg noodle; hence *yakisoba,* or "grilled noodles." My take on the Japanese street-food favorite uses a generous portion of garlic and shallots to build the flavor base, along with a pair of savory Japanese sauces — mirin and ponzu. Cabbage, carrots, and chicken simmer in the sauces, infusing the concentrated liquid with even more flavor. The noodles are tossed in the delicious mixture and fried for a few minutes more, making a very quick and very tasty meal. • serves 4

Prepare the soba noodles according to package directions until al dente, then soak the noodles in an ice bath for 20 seconds once done to prevent over-cooking. Rinse, toss with 1 tablespoon of the sesame oil, and set aside.

In a small bowl, whisk together 1 tablespoon of the sesame oil, the soy sauce, ponzu, mirin, ginger, and red pepper flakes. Set aside.

Heat the canola oil and remaining 2 tablespoons sesame oil in a large wok or frying pan over medium-high heat. Add the garlic and shallots and cook, stirring occasionally, until slightly transparent, about 4 minutes. Add the chicken, carrot, and cabbage and cook, stirring occasionally, until the chicken is nearly cooked through, 5 to 8 minutes. Add the noodles and soy sauce mixture and stir to incorporate. Raise the heat to high and continue to cook, stirring occasionally, until the vegetables and chicken are cooked through, about 3 minutes. Serve immediately.

CHICKEN FRIED RICE
with Oyster Sauce

OYSTER SAUCE HAS AN INTENSE UMAMI FLAVOR that's almost pungent: It's not something you want to eat on its own, but it makes for the most fantastically savory sauce when combined with other ingredients. I combine it with vinegar and soy sauce for the base seasoning for fried rice, with green onions incorporated for a bit of a crunch and onion-like heat. Meanwhile, chicken legs and thighs are rubbed with an oyster and dark sweet soy sauce coating and roasted until golden and juicy. All of the components meld together to create a resoundingly savory and delicious fried rice. • serves 4

For the chicken, preheat the oven to 400°F.

In a medium bowl, whisk together the garlic, oyster sauce, soy sauce, dark sweet soy sauce, and sesame oil until combined. Add the chicken drumsticks and thighs and toss to coat. Place in a casserole dish and roast for 45 minutes, until the skin is crispy and the meat is cooked through. Allow to cool. Reserve the pan drippings. Remove the meat from the bones (discard the skin and bones) and finely chop the meat.

For the fried rice, bring the water to a boil in a medium saucepan over medium heat. Add the rice, reduce the heat, and cover. Simmer until the rice absorbs all of the liquid, about 20 minutes. Fluff lightly with a fork and set aside.

In a small bowl, whisk together the vinegar, sugar, oyster sauce, soy sauce, and salt until combined. Set aside.

Heat the canola oil in a large wok over high heat. Add the rice, vinegar mixture, chopped chicken, and pan drippings and stir to combine. Continue cooking over high heat, stirring every 30 seconds, for 5 minutes, until the rice absorbs the vinegar mixture. Add the green onions and cook, stirring occasionally, for 1 minute more. Remove from the heat and serve.

Roasted Chicken

4 garlic cloves, minced

1 tablespoon oyster sauce

2 teaspoons soy sauce

1 teaspoon dark sweet soy sauce

1 teaspoon sesame oil

10 ounces chicken drumsticks (about 2)

1 pound chicken thighs (about 2), bone in and skin on

Fried Rice

4 cups water

2 cups uncooked white rice

¼ cup rice vinegar

3 tablespoons granulated sugar

1 tablespoon oyster sauce

2 teaspoons soy sauce

1 teaspoon kosher salt

1 tablespoon canola oil

2 green onions, thinly sliced

Homemade Chicken Breakfast Sausage

1⅓ pounds boneless skinless chicken thighs

3 tablespoons light brown sugar

1½ teaspoons rubbed dried sage

1 teaspoon kosher salt

½ teaspoon dried rosemary

½ teaspoon freshly cracked black pepper

¼ teaspoon ground cayenne pepper

¼ teaspoon dried thyme

1 teaspoon unsalted butter, lard, or shortening (optional, for making sausage links)

4 feet goat casing (optional, for making sausage links)

1 tablespoon extra virgin olive oil

I'D NEVER TRIED MAKING SAUSAGE before writing this book, and I was honestly surprised by how easy it was. Once you get the right equipment, the process is very simple. I bought a meat grinder and sausage stuffer attachment for my stand mixer, but you can also purchase those as stand-alone pieces. It's a bit addicting after you start, because you realize you have the freedom to stuff your sausage with absolutely anything, opening the door to a wide range of possibilities. Here, chicken thighs are ground and mixed with brown sugar, sage, rosemary, cayenne, and other seasonings. Goat casing is used for these sausages because it's smaller than pork casing, making the perfect size for breakfast sausages. The result of your labor is a salty, sweet, herbal, and juicy breakfast sausage that beats the pork version by a mile. • makes about 1½ pounds sausage

---

Use a meat grinder set to the fine grinding setting to grind the chicken thighs into a medium bowl. Alternatively, you can use the blade attachment of a food processor to grind the meat, pulsing until ground smooth and emptying the mixture into a medium bowl.

Add the brown sugar, sage, salt, rosemary, black pepper, cayenne, and thyme to the bowl and knead with your hands until the seasonings are evenly distributed. Cover and refrigerate for 30 minutes.

If making sausage links: Prep your sausage stuffer by greasing the exterior of the small size stuffing tube with butter, lard, or shortening. Gently pull the casing onto the stuffing tube until there's only a few inches left of casing and tie off the end.

Use the sausage stuffer according to the manufacturer's directions, stuffing the casing so that the sausage appears plump but has plenty of give when you squeeze gently. Be extra careful not to overstuff as goat casing is thinner and more temperamental than pork casing. Use a toothpick to poke small holes in the casing if any air bubbles appear in the sausage. When the casing has been stuffed with all of the filling, cut it off a few inches from the filling and tie it off. Go 4 inches down the sausage and pinch with your thumb and forefinger to create a flat space in the sausage. Twist the sausage 3 times towards you and repeat again 4 inches further down the sausage, this time twisting the sausage away from you. Repeat until you have created links all the way down the sausage.

Wrap in plastic wrap and refrigerate in an airtight container for up to 2 days. You can also boil them for 10 minutes and cool, then refrigerate in an airtight container for up to 1 week. You can also freeze them, boiled, in a freezer-safe airtight container for up to 6 months.

To cook the link sausages, heat the olive oil and ½ inch of water in a medium frying pan over medium-high heat. Add the sausages, working in batches if necessary, and simmer until the liquid has evaporated from the pan and the sausages are golden brown, turning them as needed to brown evenly.

If making sausage patties: Form handfuls of the chicken mixture between the palms of your hands into roughly 3-inch patties. Heat the olive oil in a medium frying pan over medium heat. Working in batches as necessary, add the patties and fry until golden brown on each side and cooked through, 4 to 5 minutes per side.

To freeze the uncooked patties, stack with a piece of parchment paper between each and store in an airtight freezer-safe container for up to 6 months.

Homemade Chicken and Apple Sausage

1 sweet apple (such as Fuji), peeled, cored, and diced

½ small yellow onion, diced

1 pound boneless skinless chicken breasts

1 pound boneless skinless chicken thighs

2 tablespoons dark brown sugar

2 teaspoons minced fresh rosemary leaves

1¼ teaspoons kosher salt

½ teaspoon rubbed dried sage

½ teaspoon dried savory

¼ teaspoon cinnamon

¼ teaspoon cloves

1 teaspoon unsalted butter, lard, or shortening (optional, for making sausage links)

4 feet pork casing (optional, for making sausage links)

1 tablespoon extra virgin olive oil

I BLEND WHITE AND DARK MEAT CHICKEN WITH APPLE and onion to make this savory sausage. Rosemary, cinnamon, sage, and cloves help bring out the sweetness of the apple, and dried savory complements the chicken and onion. Savory is often used in chicken soups, but here it provides a wonderful cooler herbal counterpoint to the warmer spices and seasonings. To make link sausages, you'll need a sausage stuffer and fresh pork casings (which you can find in the butcher department of most organic supermarkets). Lacking a stuffer and casings, you can simply form the sausage mixture into patties and fry them up in a pan. Either way, you'll enjoy a juicy, sweet, and savory flavor that I've not yet encountered in any other sausage. • makes about 2½ pounds sausage

Using a meat grinder set to the fine grinding setting, grind the apple, onion, and chicken breasts and thighs, into a medium bowl. Alternatively, you can use the blade attachment of a food processor to grind all the chicken, apple, and onion, pulsing until ground smooth and emptying the mixture into a medium bowl.

Add the brown sugar, rosemary, salt, sage, savory, cinnamon, and cloves to the bowl and knead with your hands until the seasonings are evenly distributed. Cover and refrigerate for 30 minutes.

If making sausage links: Prep your sausage stuffer by greasing the exterior of the standard size stuffing tube with butter, lard, or shortening. Gently pull the casing onto the stuffing tube until there's only a few inches left of casing, then tie off the end.

Use the sausage stuffer according to the manufacturer's directions, stuffing the casing so that the sausage appears plump but has plenty of give when you squeeze it gently. Use a toothpick to poke small holes in the casing if air bubbles appear in the sausage. When the casing has been stuffed with all of the filling, cut it off a few inches from the filling and tie it off. Go 6 inches down the sausage and pinch with your thumb and forefinger to create a flat space in the sausage. Twist the sausage 3 times towards you. Repeat again 6 inches further down the sausage and this time twist the sausage away from you. Repeat until you have created links all the way down the sausage.

Wrap in plastic wrap and refrigerate in an airtight container for up to 2 days. You can also boil them for 10 minutes and cool, then refrigerate in an airtight container for up to 1 week. You can also freeze them, boiled, in a freezer-safe airtight container for up to 6 months.

To cook the link sausages, heat the olive oil and 1 inch of water in a medium frying pan over medium-high heat. Add the sausages, working in batches if necessary, and simmer until the liquid has evaporated from the pan and the sausages are golden brown, turning them as needed to brown evenly.

If making sausage patties: Form handfuls of the chicken, apple, and spice mixture between the palms of your hands into roughly 4-inch patties. Heat the olive oil in a medium frying pan over medium heat. Working in batches as necessary, add the patties and fry until golden brown on each side and cooked through, 4 to 5 minutes per side.

To freeze the uncooked patties, stack with a piece of parchment paper between each and store in an airtight freezer-safe container for up to 6 months.

Sausage-Stuffed Savory French Toast
with Grey-Eye Gravy

Stuffing and Gravy

6 tablespoons (¾ stick) unsalted butter

½ large yellow onion, diced

6 ounces Homemade Chicken Breakfast Sausage (page 128), removed from casings (if any)

¼ cup plus 1 tablespoon all-purpose flour

1⅓ cups chicken stock

⅓ cup brewed Earl Grey tea

1 tablespoon bourbon whiskey

½ teaspoon garlic powder

½ teaspoon onion powder

½ teaspoon rubbed dried sage

½ teaspoon freshly cracked black pepper

Kosher salt to taste

French Toast

3 cups milk

4 large eggs

1 tablespoon chopped fresh thyme leaves

1 tablespoon chopped fresh rosemary leaves

1 tablespoon chopped fresh sage leaves

2 teaspoons kosher salt

1 teaspoon freshly cracked black pepper

½ teaspoon garlic powder

½ teaspoon onion powder

8 (½-inch-thick) French bread slices, left out overnight

STUFFED FRENCH TOAST IS A LOT EASIER TO MAKE than you might imagine. You basically slice the bread a bit thinner than you would for regular French toast, soak in a custard base, and then sandwich a filling between two slices, pressing the edges together to create a gloriously stuffed piece of bread. I give them a savory twist here and use a chicken breakfast sausage and onion stuffing, then top with an herbed rich "grey-eye gravy" made from chicken stock and Earl Grey tea, a flavorful take on red-eye gravy, which traditionally contains a coffee base. The result is an incredible mix of flavors that beats out sweet French toast any day of the week. • serves 4

For the stuffing, melt ¼ cup of the butter in a large frying pan over medium heat. Add the onion and cook, stirring occasionally, until translucent and golden around the edges, about 15 minutes. Add the sausage and cook, stirring occasionally, until cooked through, breaking the meat apart with the end of your spoon as it cooks. Use a slotted spoon to transfer the sausage and onion to a separate plate and set them aside.

For the gravy, add the remaining 2 tablespoons butter to the pan and allow it to melt completely. Add the flour and whisk until a thick paste forms. Add the stock, ⅓ cup at a time, then the tea and bourbon, whisking constantly, until a smooth gravy forms. Add the garlic powder, onion powder, sage, and black pepper, stir to combine, and taste. Add salt as desired. Cover and set aside.

For the French toast, place a baking sheet in the oven and preheat the oven to 250°F.

In a large bowl, whisk together the milk, eggs, thyme, rosemary, sage, salt, black pepper, garlic powder, and onion powder until completely combined. Begin heating a well-greased griddle.

Empty the milk mixture into a wide shallow dish. Working in batches if necessary, add the bread slices, allowing them to soak in the mixture for 5 minutes, turning once. Before removing each slice, gently pat it over the bowl to allow excess liquid to drip off, taking care not to tear the bread. Lay 4 slices flat on a clean work surface and spread about 2 tablespoons of the sausage stuffing mixture over the center of each slice. Place another piece of soaked bread on top of each one and gently pinch the edges together to create a seal around the filling.

Place the sealed French toast on the hot greased griddle and cook, turning once, until deeply golden brown on both sides, 4 to 6 minutes per side. As they finish cooking, transfer them to the baking sheet in the oven so that they stay warm.

Once all the French toast is prepared, place them on a serving platter and top with the gravy. Serve immediately.

Soups & Braises

Mulligatawny Soup

Boring chicken stew, this isn't! A stick-to-your-ribs dish, this mulligatawny soup will warm you from the inside out with a creamy richness that still delivers a healthy serving of protein and veggies. Cumin, ginger, curry powder, and cloves are just a few of the mélange of spices found in this English-Indian classic. Chicken gizzards are also used here; you can find them pretty easily near the chicken at most supermarkets. If not, you can also substitute an equal amount of chicken thighs instead. • serves 6

Melt the butter in a large pot over medium heat. Add the chicken thighs and cook until lightly browned on each side. Add the gizzards and cook, stirring occasionally, for another 5 minutes. Remove both the chicken thighs and gizzards from the pot and set aside. Remove the thigh meat from the bone and cut into 1-inch pieces.

Add the onion, garlic, cloves, and bay leaf to the pot and cook, stirring, until the onion is translucent, about 5 minutes. Add the carrots, leek, mushrooms, ½ cup of the stock, the curry powder, ginger, salt, black pepper, cumin, and allspice and cook uncovered, stirring occasionally, for 15 minutes.

Add the chicken, gizzards, remaining 7½ cups stock, and the rice to the pot. Reduce the heat to low, cover, and simmer for 30 minutes. Remove from the heat and stir in the yogurt and cream until smooth. Serve immediately.

⅓ cup unsalted butter

1⅓ pounds large chicken thighs, bone in and skin on

¾ pound chicken gizzards

1 large yellow onion, diced

7 garlic cloves, minced

¼ teaspoon whole cloves

1 bay leaf

2 carrots, peeled and sliced

1 leek, white and light green parts, washed well, sliced

3 ounces cremini mushrooms, diced

8 cups chicken stock

2 tablespoons curry powder

1 tablespoon grated fresh ginger

1½ teaspoons kosher salt

1 teaspoon freshly cracked black pepper

¾ teaspoon cumin

¼ teaspoon allspice

¾ cup uncooked basmati rice

1⅓ cups plain full-fat or low-fat yogurt

½ cup heavy cream

CHICKEN MUSHROOM SOUP

¼ cup extra virgin olive oil

¾ pound boneless skinless chicken thighs, cut into 1-inch cubes

2 medium yellow onions, chopped

8 ounces shiitake mushrooms, cut into ½-inch-thick slices

4 ounces chanterelle mushrooms, cut into ½-inch-thick slices

3 cups chicken stock

1 tablespoon plus 2 teaspoons Hungarian paprika

1 tablespoon soy sauce

2 teaspoons minced fresh dill

1 teaspoon fresh thyme leaves

1 teaspoon minced fresh marjoram

½ teaspoon freshly cracked black pepper

3 tablespoons unsalted butter

¼ cup all-purpose flour

1 cup whole milk

1 tablespoon freshly squeezed lemon juice

⅔ cup sour cream

Kosher salt to taste

CHANTERELLE AND SHIITAKE MUSHROOMS COMBINE with chicken in this fantastic savory soup. Thyme, marjoram, and dill add a comforting element, while paprika contributes a sweet and subtle kick of flavor. The broth is thickened with a bit of milk, butter, flour, and sour cream to create a rich and cozy soup that's perfect for cool winter evenings. • serves 4

Heat the olive oil in a large frying pan over medium heat. Add the chicken and onions and cook, stirring occasionally, until the onions are translucent and the chicken is lightly cooked on all sides, about 8 minutes. Add the mushrooms, 1 cup chicken stock, paprika, soy sauce, dill, thyme, marjoram, and black pepper. Simmer, stirring occasionally, until the mushrooms soften and become dark in color, about 15 minutes.

Melt the butter in a large Dutch oven over medium heat. Whisk in the flour and continue whisking while the mixture cooks for another 3 minutes. Add the milk and reduce the heat to medium low. Continue cooking, stirring once every minute or so, until the mixture thickens, about 10 minutes. Empty the mushroom mixture into the milk mixture. Stir in the lemon juice and the remainder of the chicken stock. Cover and simmer over low heat for 20 minutes, until very fragrant with the smell of mushrooms.

Remove from the heat and watch the mixture until it stops simmering. When it ceases, stir in the sour cream. Add salt to taste and serve.

Avgolemono Soup

1 small chicken (about 2½ pounds)

1 large yellow onion, chopped

3 teaspoons kosher salt

3 lemons

3 tablespoons extra virgin olive oil

2 teaspoons minced fresh oregano leaves

1 teaspoon freshly cracked black pepper

¾ cup orzo pasta or uncooked white rice

3 large eggs, whites and yolks separated

NOTHING MAKES ME FEEL WARM inside and out like a hot bowl of avgolemono soup. The Greeks' version of chicken soup, avgolemono is made from chicken broth, eggs, and fresh-squeezed lemon juice. The eggs are separated and the whites are beaten until light and foamy. Then the yolks and lemon juice are whisked in and the entire mixture is slowly incorporated into a rich broth. This creates a thick and silky texture (the best way to describe it is "liquid velvet") and makes for an unforgettably savory soup. • serves 6

Remove the skin from the chicken. Place the remaining chicken and the onion in a medium pot and add just enough water to barely cover the bird. Add 1 teaspoon of the salt and bring to a boil. Boil the bird until it is cooked through, about an hour, skimming off any froth that appears on top of the broth every 10 minutes with a mesh spoon and discarding it.

Preheat the oven to broil.

Remove the chicken from the broth and place in an oven-proof pan, breast facing up. Use a slotted spoon to take out the onion and place around the chicken in the pan. Set aside the pot with the broth.

In a small bowl, mix together the juice from 1 of the lemons, the olive oil, 1 teaspoon of the oregano, 1 teaspoon of the salt, ½ teaspoon of the black pepper. Drizzle over the chicken and the onion. Place the pan in the oven and broil the chicken for 15 minutes, until it is lightly golden on top.

Meanwhile, add 2 cups of water and the remaining 1 teaspoon salt to the broth in the pot and bring back to a boil. Add the orzo or rice and cook until cooked all the way through, 10 minutes for orzo and 15 minutes for rice. Remove the pot from the heat and set aside.

In a medium bowl, whisk the egg whites at high speed until a foam forms on top. Whisk in the egg yolks and the juice from the remaining two lemons until fully incorporated.

Make sure the broth has sat at room temperature off the heat source for about 10 minutes before this next step. Slowly ladle hot broth into the lemon-egg mixture, whisking all the while. Continue adding the broth until 2 cups of the broth have been incorporated into the lemon-egg mixture. The broth should be slightly thick and frothy at this point. Whisk the lemon-egg mixture into the large pot of broth until fully mixed. Add the remaining 1 teaspoon oregano and ½ teaspoon black pepper, taste, and add more salt and pepper if you'd like. Serve warm with the broiled chicken on the side.

Tom Kha Gai

I'M NOT USUALLY ONE FOR EATING SOUP in the summertime, but the brightness and comfortingly fresh flavors of this Thai soup are especially wonderful during the hot summer months with fresh summer tomato in the broth. It's a creamy soup with a coconut milk base and the deep flavors of galangal, kaffir lime leaf, lemongrass, mushrooms, tomato, and chicken. You can find fresh kaffir lime leaves and galangal at many Asian markets; or look for dried leaves online — they pack the same amount of flavor. • serves 6

In a large pot, bring the coconut milk, stock, and water to a boil over medium-high heat. Add the onion, galangal, and lemongrass and reduce the heat to medium low. Simmer until the soup becomes very fragrant and the onion has softened slightly, about 5 minutes.

Stir in the chicken, mushrooms, and tomato and simmer until the chicken is cooked through, about 5 minutes. Add the fish sauce, soy sauce, sugar, and coriander and stir until combined. Remove from the heat and stir in the lime juice, kaffir lime leaves, and green onions. Allow the soup to rest for 5 minutes. Add salt to taste as needed and serve immediately.

4 cups full-fat coconut milk

2 cups chicken stock

2 cups water

1 medium yellow onion, thickly sliced

⅓ cup dried sliced galangal root

1 stalk lemongrass, cut into 1-inch pieces

1 pound boneless skinless chicken breasts, cut into ½-inch-thick slices

3 ounces sliced cremini or shiitake mushrooms

1 large tomato, cut into eighths

3 tablespoons fish sauce

1 tablespoon soy sauce

2 teaspoons palm or coconut sugar

½ teaspoon ground coriander

3 tablespoons freshly squeezed lime juice

4 kaffir lime leaves

4 green onions, sliced

Kosher salt to taste

Chicken Udon Noodle Soup

THE KEY TO A GOOD UDON SOUP is a layered and rich broth, and this recipe doesn't fail to deliver. Dried shiitake mushrooms are soaked in warm water to create an intense, umami-rich stock. Dashi, a Japanese fish stock, is added along with other seasonings to create a complex and deeply satisfying broth. The chicken is simmered in the broth to add to the flavor of the dish, but the fresh vegetables are added at the end, which keeps them nice and crisp, contrasting with the soft and gummy udon noodles. Add a soft-poached egg or two and you have yourself a truly delicious soup. • serves 2

10 dried shiitake mushrooms

5½ cups warm water

1 tablespoon plus 2 teaspoons mirin

1 tablespoon soy sauce

2 teaspoons ponzu

2 teaspoons powdered dashi base

1 teaspoon rice vinegar

1 pound boneless skinless chicken breasts, cut into 1-inch cubes

1 large carrot, peeled and cut into ¼-inch-thick slices

3 ounces oyster mushrooms

1½ ounces fresh shiitake mushrooms

5 ounces dried udon noodles

4 green onions, thinly sliced

1 large radish or 3 small radishes, thinly sliced

2 ounces radicchio, sliced

2 large eggs

In a medium bowl, place the dried shiitake mushrooms in 1½ cups of the warm water and soak for 30 minutes. Remove the mushrooms, dice, and set aside.

Empty the mushroom soaking water into a medium pot and add the remaining 4 cups water. Place the pot over medium-high heat and stir in the mirin, soy sauce, ponzu, dashi base, and rice vinegar. Bring to a boil. Add the chicken breasts and reduce the heat. Cover and simmer, stirring once, until the chicken is cooked through, about 6 minutes. Add the carrot, oyster mushrooms, fresh shiitake mushrooms, and rehydrated shiitake mushrooms and simmer for an additional 5 minutes. Cover and set aside.

Fill a separate medium stockpot about two-thirds full with water and bring to a boil. Add the udon noodles and boil, stirring every 4 minutes, until cooked through, about 10 minutes. Drain, rinse with cold water, and drain again. Add the noodles to the broth in the medium pot and stir in the green onions, radish, and radicchio. Crack the eggs over the top of the pot, cover, and simmer over low heat until the whites of the eggs are cooked but the yolks are still soft and jiggly, about 4 minutes. Serve immediately.

CHICKEN CORN CHOWDER

6 cups Smoky Chicken Giblet Stock (page 268)

1¾ pounds large chicken breasts, bone in and skin on

4 tablespoons unsalted butter

1 large yellow onion, diced

2 shallots, diced

3 garlic cloves, minced

¼ cup all-purpose flour

2 cups fresh corn kernels

2 medium Yukon gold potatoes, peeled and cut into 1-inch cubes

2 teaspoons fresh thyme leaves

1½ teaspoons finely chopped fresh rosemary leaves

1 teaspoon soy sauce

½ teaspoon freshly cracked black pepper

Kosher salt to taste

THIS HEARTY TAKE ON THE CORN CLASSIC uses a homemade smoky stock to add another layer of flavor to the creamy, sweet, and savory chowder. Bone-in chicken breasts are simmered with fresh corn kernels, onion, shallots, garlic, potatoes, and rosemary to create a thick and silky soup that's packed with flavor. • serves 6

Bring the stock to a boil over medium heat. Add the chicken breasts and reduce the heat to low. Cover and simmer until just cooked through, 25 to 30 minutes. Remove the chicken and set it aside on a separate plate to cool, then peel the skin off the chicken and remove the meat from the bone by gently easing your fingers underneath the breast meat to peel it off the bone in one large piece. Discard the bones and skin. Cut the meat into 1-inch pieces. Remove the stockpot from the heat and set it aside.

Melt the butter in a large Dutch oven over medium-low heat. Add the onion, shallots, and garlic and bring the heat up to medium. Cook, stirring every 5 to 10 minutes, until the onion is golden brown and caramelized, 30 to 45 minutes depending on the heat of your stovetop.

Add the flour and stir until incorporated. Toast in the pan, stirring to keep it from burning, for 2 minutes. Whisk in 1 cup of the stock until the flour mixture has integrated into the stock and a smooth thick liquid forms. Add the remaining stock, the chicken breast meat, corn, potatoes, thyme, rosemary, soy sauce, and pepper. Reduce the heat to low and simmer, stirring every 10 minutes, until the chowder is thickened and the potatoes are cooked through, about 30 minutes. Add salt to taste and serve immediately.

BRAISED CHICKEN
with Pineapple–Sour Cream Curry

I HEARD ABOUT THIS RECIPE FROM A RESORT MANAGER I met while travelling for work in the British Virgin Islands. He talked about a delicious pineapple and sour cream curry that a former employer made, and I knew that I had to re-create it for this book. It has a pretty simple ingredient list as far as curries go, and that's because the pineapple, curry powder, sour cream, and chicken hold up the dish on their own. The sweet, tangy, creamy spiced flavor permeates the tender meat and creates an incredibly comforting dish that a home cook of any level can easily prepare. • serves 4

2 tablespoons unsalted butter

1 teaspoon minced fresh ginger

4 garlic cloves, minced

4 boneless skinless chicken thighs (about 1 pound)

1 pound fresh peeled and cored pineapple, cut into 1-inch cubes

1 cup chicken stock

3 tablespoons light brown sugar

2 teaspoons curry powder

½ teaspoon red Thai curry paste

¼ teaspoon turmeric

¾ cup sour cream

½ cup coarsely chopped red bell pepper

1 tablespoon freshly squeezed lime juice

Kosher salt to taste

4 cups prepared basmati rice

2 tablespoons fresh cilantro leaves, for garnish (optional)

Preheat the oven to 375°F.

Melt the butter in a medium Dutch oven over medium heat. Add the ginger and garlic and cook, stirring occasionally, until fragrant, about 3 minutes. Add the chicken thighs and cook until lightly browned on both sides. Set aside.

Add the pineapple, stock, brown sugar, curry powder, red curry paste, and turmeric and stir to combine. Reduce the heat and simmer until the sauce turns a deep yellow and the liquid reduces by about a fourth, about 10 minutes. Push the pineapple to the sides of the pan to make space for the chicken. Nestle the thighs in the pot and cover. Transfer to the oven and braise for 1 hour to 1 hour 15 minutes, until the chicken has cooked through and is very tender and the pineapple has nearly disintegrated.

Remove the pot from the oven and place over low heat on the stovetop. Add the sour cream, bell pepper, and lime juice and stir until combined. Taste and add salt as desired. Raise the heat to medium and simmer for an additional 3 minutes to soften the pepper slightly. Garnish with fresh cilantro leaves, if desired. Serve alongside the basmati rice.

Braised Chicken Quarters
with Morels, Tarragon, and Brown Butter

1 ounce dried morel mushrooms

2 cups warm water

2 tablespoons unsalted butter

1 large shallot, diced

3 garlic cloves, minced

½ teaspoon kosher salt

2 ounces shiitake mushrooms, thinly sliced

1 tablespoon minced fresh tarragon leaves

2 chicken leg quarters (about ¾ pound each), bone in and skin on

1 teaspoon heavy cream

2 teaspoons fresh thyme leaves

IF YOU'VE NEVER HAD MORELS, you're in for a real treat. Nutty, earthy, and wonderfully soft, these mushrooms feature small crater-like pockets that make the perfect folds for catching and holding sauce, which happens to be brown butter in this dish. Fresh morels are usually only found in the spring at farmers' markets, but you can find dried morels any time of the year at most natural food stores. I use dried morels here, and after a bit of rehydrating, they taste just as savory as the fresh ones. They can be a bit expensive out of season, so you could also substitute other mushroom varieties if you'd like, but nothing tastes quite like morels. Plus you're left with a delicious broth, which is incorporated into the chicken cooking liquid that's spooned over the chicken legs while they're simmering, making for a luxuriously rich and deeply flavorful dinner. • serves 2

Soak the morels in the warm water until rehydrated and softened, about 15 minutes. Reserve the soaking liquid and the morels separately.

Meanwhile, melt the butter over medium heat in a stainless steel medium frying pan. Add the shallot, garlic, and salt and cook, stirring occasionally, until the shallot becomes slightly translucent, about 4 minutes. Add the morels, shiitakes, and tarragon and cook, stirring every 2 minutes, until the shiitake have darkened in color and wrinkled slightly and the butter turns a deep golden hue and smells slightly nutty, about 8 minutes. Remove the shallot, garlic, morels, and mushrooms with a slotted spoon and set them aside.

Add the chicken leg quarters to the pan. Cook until well browned on both sides, then flip them skin side up and add the reserved morel soaking liquid so that it comes up to about 1 inch in the pan. Simmer over medium heat until the liquid in the pan has reduced by at least half and the chicken is cooked through, 1 hour to 1 hour 20 minutes, spooning the simmering liquid over the chicken every 10 minutes.

Add the cream and whisk into the pan juices. Return the morel mixture to the pan along with the fresh thyme and stir to coat in the sauce. Serve immediately.

Lemon and Olive Chicken Tagine

A tagine is a ceramic cooking vessel with a cone-shaped lid that allows evaporating steam to condense and run down the sides of the cone and back into the simmering stew — essentially a self-basting pot. It's perfect for cooking chicken because it keeps in all the savory juices, and when you add sweet and bitter elements like dates, lemon, and olives you get an delicious, flavor-packed stew. You can serve it on its own, or with a little rice to help stretch the flavorful broth. (The flavor is so good I tend to sip down all the broth immediately and then I don't have any left to dip the chicken and veggies in. A true tragedy.) If you don't have access to a tagine, you can also use a cast iron Dutch oven that has a securely fitting lid. • serves 2

Melt the butter in a large tagine or cast iron Dutch oven over medium heat. In a small bowl, mix together the salt, cinnamon, turmeric, black pepper, cumin, and mace. Coat the chicken with the spice mixture and cook in the butter until browned on both sides. It's okay if it's not cooked completely through at this point. Remove from the tagine and set aside. Add the onion and garlic to the tagine and cook, stirring occasionally, until slightly translucent, around 5 minutes. Add the ginger and cook, stirring occasionally, for 2 minutes more.

Add the cauliflower, lemon, stock, olives, and dates and stir to combine. Push the contents of the tagine to the side to make room for the chicken breasts. Place them back in and cover with the tagine top. Reduce the heat to low and simmer until the chicken is cooked through, 35 to 40 minutes. Serve.

3 tablespoons unsalted butter

1½ teaspoons kosher salt

1 teaspoon ground cinnamon

¾ teaspoon turmeric

½ teaspoon freshly cracked black pepper

¼ teaspoon cumin

¼ teaspoon mace

2 large chicken breasts (about 2½ pounds), bone in and skin on

1 red onion, diced

4 garlic cloves, crushed

1 tablespoon minced fresh ginger

1 small head cauliflower or romanesco broccoli (about 1 pound), broken into roughly 2-inch chunks

1 lemon, quartered

½ cup chicken stock

½ cup pitted green olives

½ cup chopped pitted dates

HERBED CHICKEN
with Garlic and Rosemary Dumplings

Herbed Chicken

4 tablespoons unsalted butter

1 large sweet onion, diced

3 garlic cloves, minced

3 small Yukon gold potatoes, peeled and cut into 1-inch cubes

4 carrots, peeled and cut into ¼-inch-thick slices

1 small turnip, peeled, quartered, and cut into ¼-inch-thick slices

1 bay leaf

⅓ cup all-purpose flour

2 cups chicken stock

2 teaspoons fresh thyme leaves

2 teaspoons minced fresh rosemary leaves

4 chicken thighs (about 1¾ pounds), bone in and skin on

Garlic and Rosemary Dumplings

¾ cup plus 1 tablespoon all-purpose flour

1¾ teaspoons baking powder

1 teaspoon minced fresh rosemary

½ teaspoon kosher salt

¼ teaspoon freshly cracked black pepper

⅔ cup whole or low-fat milk

2 garlic cloves, minced

ROSEMARY IS MY FAVORITE HERB IN THE WORLD because it tastes so good in both savory and sweet dishes. Here it kicks the traditional chicken and dumplings up a notch, by being infused into the dough of the dumplings (in addition to minced garlic). The chicken is simmered in a rich broth built from a variety of fresh vegetables and herbs, and the dumplings are dropped into the broth and simmered in the flavorful juices until puffy and cooked through. This recipe calls for dark meat (chicken thighs) but you can substitute chicken breasts if you're more of a white meat fan. • serves 4

———————————————————

For the chicken, melt the butter in a Dutch oven over medium heat. Add the onion and garlic and cook, stirring occasionally, for 3 minutes. Add the potatoes, carrots, turnip, and bay leaf and cook, stirring occasionally, for 10 minutes. Add the flour and stir until incorporated. Stir in the stock, thyme, and rosemary. Nestle the chicken thighs into the pot and reduce the heat to low. Simmer, uncovered, stirring every 10 minutes, for 30 minutes.

For the dumplings, in a bowl, mix together the flour, baking powder, rosemary, salt, and pepper. Gradually add the milk, stirring as you pour, until a soft dough forms. Stir in the garlic.

Drop the dumpling dough into the simmering pot in 6 heaping spoonfuls, spacing them out equally since they will swell as they cook. Cover and simmer until the dumplings are plump and the chicken is cooked through, 15 to 20 minutes. Discard the bay leaf. Serve immediately.

Red Thai Chicken Curry

When I'm feeling under the weather, my appetite pretty much disintegrates and there's not much I want or feel like eating. The only exception is red chicken curry, which I will eat at any time of the day or night, in sickness and in health. There is just something about creamy and subtly sweet coconut milk paired with pleasantly spicy curry paste that creates the perfect combination of heat and richness, each one bringing out the best of the other. • serves 2

In a medium saucepan, bring the coconut milk and curry paste to a simmer over medium-low heat. Cook, stirring every minute, for 5 minutes. Add the chicken, sugar, water, tomato, garlic, lemongrass, fish sauce, and salt and simmer, stirring every 2 to 3 minutes, for 10 minutes, until the tomatoes soften and the mixture is very aromatic. Add the bell pepper and simmer until very slightly tender, stirring every minute, for an additional 5 minutes. Add the basil and lime juice and stir for 1 minute. Serve alongside the jasmine rice.

2 (13.5-ounce) cans full-fat coconut milk

1½ tablespoons red curry paste

1 large (½-pound) boneless skinless chicken breast, cut into ½-inch-thick slices

¼ cup palm sugar or light brown sugar

¼ cup water

1 medium tomato, cut into 6 slices

4 garlic cloves, minced

1 (2-inch) piece lemongrass, thinly sliced

1 tablespoon fish sauce

¼ teaspoon kosher salt

1 large red bell pepper, sliced

6 fresh Thai basil or Italian basil leaves

2 teaspoons freshly squeezed lime juice or 1 kaffir lime leaf

3 cups prepared jasmine rice

Chicken Tikka Masala

Marinade and Chicken

1 cup plain full-fat yogurt

1 teaspoon tomato paste

1 garlic clove, minced

½ teaspoon grated fresh ginger

½ teaspoon freshly cracked black pepper

¼ teaspoon cumin

¼ teaspoon cayenne

1 pound large boneless skinless chicken breasts (about 2)

Tikka Masala

4 tablespoons ghee or clarified butter

1 tablespoon extra virgin olive oil

2 tablespoons plus 1 teaspoon tomato paste

8 garlic cloves, minced

1 tablespoon freshly grated fresh ginger

9 plum tomatoes, diced

1 serrano chile, seeded and diced

1 teaspoon garam masala

½ teaspoon cumin

½ teaspoon cayenne pepper

½ teaspoon paprika

¼ teaspoon cinnamon

¼ teaspoon cardamom

1½ cups chicken stock

⅓ cup heavy cream

Kosher salt to taste

Naan, or prepared basmati rice, for serving

THIS IS MY ABSOLUTE FAVORITE INDIAN RECIPE. There's just something about garlic, spices, tomatoes, and cream that is supremely comforting and flavorful without being overpowering. I use garam masala in this recipe, which is a traditional Indian spice that you can find at any Indian market and in the ethnic foods section of most major grocery stores. If you cannot find ghee, substitute clarified unsalted butter, but there's something about the intrinsically nutty and savory flavor of ghee that's almost cheese-like and adds another level of depth to the dish, so I recommend using it if you can. • serves 4

To marinate the chicken, in a medium bowl, mix together the yogurt, tomato paste, garlic, ginger, black pepper, cumin, and cayenne until smooth. Toss the chicken breasts in the mixture until coated. Place the chicken breasts and marinade in a resealable plastic bag, squeeze as much air as possible out of the bag, and seal it. Refrigerate for at least 4 hours or overnight.

Heat a gas grill to medium heat or heat a grill pan over medium heat on the stovetop. Remove the chicken from the bag (discard the marinade). Grill until cooked through and light char-grill marks appear on both sides of the chicken. Let cool slightly. When cool enough to handle, cut the chicken into roughly 2-inch cubes and set aside.

For the tikka masala, in a large pot, melt the ghee with the oil over medium-high heat. Toast the tomato paste in the ghee and oil for 3 minutes. Add the garlic and ginger and cook, stirring, for 3 minutes. Add the tomatoes, chile, garam masala, cumin, cayenne, paprika, cinnamon, and cardamom and cook, stirring, for 3 more minutes. Add the stock and simmer until the mixture has thickened slightly, about 30 minutes.

Let cool slightly before emptying into a blender or food processor and blending until smooth. Pour the pureed mixture back into the pot and place over medium heat. Add the chicken and simmer until the flavors steep into the meat, about 30 minutes. Add the cream and stir to combine. Salt to taste and serve alongside naan or rice.

Coq au Vin

2 tablespoons unsalted butter

3 large strips bacon, cut into ½-inch squares

6 ounces frozen pearl onions (about 2½ cups)

4 pounds chicken legs and thighs, bone in and skin on

¼ cup plus 2 tablespoons all-purpose flour

½ teaspoon kosher salt

3 ounces brown or button mushrooms, cut into ½-inch-thick slices

2½ cups chicken stock

1 cup dry red wine

1½ tablespoons fresh thyme leaves or 1¾ teaspoons dried thyme

1 tablespoon tomato paste

2 bay leaves

¼ cup heavy cream

2 large carrots, peeled and cut into 2-inch pieces

1 yellow onion, quartered

7 garlic cloves, thinly sliced

Kosher salt to taste

COQ AU VIN IS A TRADITIONAL FRENCH RECIPE that translates simply as "chicken in wine." The chicken is pan-fried in butter and bacon drippings and then braised in a red wine, mushroom, and onion-based sauce. The aroma that fills your home is worth the effort of coq au vin all on its own, but the flavor of this succulent bird lives up to its aroma. Savory, rich, and comforting coq au vin will convince even the most unadventurous cooks of the delights of French cooking. • serves 4

Melt the butter in a large Dutch oven over medium heat. Add the bacon and cook until crispy. Remove the bacon from the pot and set it aside on a plate lined with paper towels, leaving the reserved fat in the pot. Add the pearl onions to the pot and cook, stirring every 3 to 5 minutes, until lightly browned, 15 to 20 minutes. Remove the pearl onions from the pot and set aside.

Toss the chicken in ¼ cup of the flour and the salt until lightly coated. Place in the pot and cook until the chicken is golden brown, about 10 minutes on each side. Remove the chicken from the pot and set it aside. Add the sliced mushrooms to the pot and cook, stirring occasionally, until they've darkened and started to wrinkle slightly, about 4 minutes. Remove the mushrooms and set aside.

Add 2 cups of the stock, the wine, thyme, tomato paste, and bay leaves to the pot and stir. Simmer until the tomato paste is evenly distributed throughout the mixture, about 5 minutes.

While it is simmering, in a separate small saucepan heat the cream over low heat, stirring constantly, until hot but not boiling. Whisk in the remaining 2 tablespoons flour until a thick paste forms. Immediately remove it from the heat and begin ladling in some of the stock from the Dutch oven, whisking the flour mixture constantly. Continue adding stock from the Dutch oven to the saucepan until the texture becomes like that of a thick gravy. Pour the contents of the saucepan into the Dutch oven and stir until evenly distributed.

Add the carrots, onion quarters, garlic, and reserved bacon. Reduce the heat and simmer until the liquid has reduced by half, about 45 minutes. Taste and add salt as needed.

Preheat the oven to 350°F.

Return the pearl onions, mushrooms, and chicken to the Dutch oven along with the remaining ½ cup stock. Place in the oven and bake for 45 minutes, basting the exposed top of the chicken thighs and legs with the pan drippings halfway through the cooking time, until the exposed chicken is golden and the vegetables are cooked through and very soft. Discard the bay leaf. Let cool for 20 minutes before serving.

CHICKEN MARSALA
with Balsamic Caramelized Onions and Pork Belly

THIS SAVORY DISH IS AN ITALIAN ONE-POT MEAL of chicken breasts coated in a deeply layered Marsala wine sauce. The sauce begins with balsamic caramelized onions, then is built up with chicken, then pork belly, then cremini and shiitake mushrooms, and finally the Marsala. Preparing everything in the same pot ensures that all the flavors from each preparation step are retained and become more and more concentrated during the cooking process, creating an exquisitely flavored dish. • serves 4

Melt with 1 tablespoon of the olive oil 1 tablespoon of the butter in a large Dutch oven over medium heat. Add the onion and reduce the heat to medium low. Cook, stirring every 5 minutes, until golden, about 20 minutes. Add the balsamic vinegar and stir to coat. Continue cooking, stirring every couple minutes, until the liquid has evaporated from the pan and the onion is a deep golden brown, about 10 minutes more. Remove the onion from the pan and set aside.

Meanwhile, place the chicken breasts between two sheets of plastic wrap and use a meat mallet to pound to an even ½-inch thickness. In a medium shallow bowl, whisk together the flour, ½ teaspoon of the salt, and ½ teaspoon of the black pepper.

Add the remaining tablespoon of butter and remaining 3 tablespoons olive oil to the Dutch oven and raise the heat to medium. Dredge the chicken breasts in the flour mixture to coat evenly. Add to the pot and cook until golden and cooked through, about 8 minutes each side. Remove from the pan and set aside.

Add the pork belly to the pot and cook, stirring occasionally, until crispy, about 5 minutes. Remove from the pot with a slotted spoon and set aside. Add the mushrooms, oregano, remaining ½ teaspoon salt, and remaining ½ teaspoon black pepper and cook, stirring occasionally, until the mushrooms have shrunk slightly and have deepened in color, about 7 minutes. Add the Marsala and stock and stir to incorporate the pan juices. Raise the heat to medium high and simmer for 5 minutes to reduce the liquid. Taste and add more salt, if needed.

Add the chicken to the pan and simmer for an additional 2 minutes. Top with the balsamic caramelized onions, salt pork belly, and fresh parsley. Serve immediately.

4 tablespoons extra virgin olive oil

2 tablespoons unsalted butter

1 large sweet onion, chopped

2 tablespoons quality balsamic vinegar

4 boneless skinless chicken breasts (about 2 pounds)

⅔ cup all-purpose flour

1 teaspoon kosher salt

1 teaspoon freshly cracked black pepper

¼ pound salt pork belly, cut into ½-inch cubes

4 ounces cremini mushrooms, cut in half

4 ounces shiitake mushrooms, cut in half

2 teaspoons minced fresh oregano leaves

½ cup Marsala wine

⅓ cup chicken stock

Kosher salt to taste
3 tablespoons coarsely chopped fresh parsley

Pastries

Chicken Empanadas

EMPANADAS ARE A TRADITIONAL ARGENTINEAN PASTRY: a flaky dough with any number of fillings. The chicken, chiles, and onion simmer along with the spices and seasonings to create a flavorful pastry that becomes more addicting with each bite. • makes about 24 empanadas

---

For the dough, in a large bowl, mix together the flour, onion powder, and salt until combined. Add the lard and pinch it with your fingers until a crumbly sand-like mixture forms. Add the egg and knead into the dough. Add the vegetable stock, 1 tablespoon at a time, kneading until a smooth dough forms. Cover and refrigerate for 30 minutes, or up to 2 days.

For the filling, heat the olive oil in a large frying pan over medium heat. Add the onion, chile, and garlic and cook, stirring occasionally, until softened and the onion becomes slightly translucent, about 4 minutes. Add the chicken, cumin, salt, ancho chili, and black pepper and stir to combine. Cook, stirring every 2 minutes, until the chicken is just cooked through, 8 to 10 minutes. Remove from the heat, stir in the eggs, and let cool to room temperature.

Preheat the oven to 375°F.

Roll out the dough on a clean and lightly floured work surface until it is about ⅛ inch thick. Use a 4-inch circular cookie cutter to cut out one dough round. Spoon about 1 heaping teaspoon of the filling onto the bottom half of the round. Dip your finger in a glass of water and trace it around the edge of the top half of the dough. Fold it over the bottom half and press the edges together to seal.

To create the *repulgue* (the braided-looking edge) start at one corner of the sealed empanada and fold the corner up over the top, pinching it together with the top once you fold it. Repeat this again with the new corner that formed at the base of the last fold and continue until sealed all the way along the edge. Place the empanada on a baking sheet. If you don't want to do the *repulgue*, you can press the edges together to seal and then roll the sealed edge up towards the filling to make the seal more secure.

Repeat with the remaining ingredients, spacing the empanadas about 2 inches apart on the baking sheet. This may take some time, so I recommend keeping a kitchen towel over the rolled-out dough to keep it from drying out and becoming unpliable.

Brush the empanadas with the egg wash and bake for 25 to 30 minutes, until puffy and golden. Let cool for 30 minutes before serving.

Dough

2½ cups plus 2 tablespoons all-purpose flour

1 teaspoon onion powder

Pinch kosher salt

½ cup lard

1 large egg, beaten

4 to 6 tablespoons vegetable stock (if using low-sodium stock add ½ teaspoon kosher salt), chilled

Filling

1 tablespoon extra virgin olive oil

1 medium yellow onion, diced

1 serrano chile, seeded and diced

2 garlic cloves, minced

½ pound boneless skinless chicken thigh, finely chopped

½ teaspoon cumin

½ teaspoon kosher salt

¼ teaspoon ancho chili powder

¼ teaspoon freshly cracked black pepper

2 hard-boiled eggs, peeled and diced

1 egg, beaten with 1 teaspoon water

Chicken, Mushroom, and Pancetta Crepes

CREPES ARE EASY TO MAKE ONCE you get the hang of them. The key is using a nonstick pan and making sure it's lightly greased and hot. The crepe should start cooking as soon as the batter hits the pan, which means you need to quickly coat the surface so you don't end up with a strange-shaped crepe (although these are just as delicious as the circular ones). For the filling, I used small mushrooms, enoki and brown beech, mixed with diced oyster mushrooms. If you're unable to locate them, however, you can use finely chopped shiitake mushrooms in their place. • serves 4

For the crepe batter, in a small bowl, mix together the flour, garlic powder, onion powder, sage, thyme, and salt. In a medium bowl, whisk together the eggs, milk, stock, and water. Add the flour mixture and whisk together until smooth. Cover and refrigerate for at least 1 hour or up to 4 hours.

For the filling, melt the butter in a large frying pan over medium-high heat. Add the chicken and cook, turning occasionally, until cooked through and browned on both sides. Set aside to cool.

Add the shallot to the pan and cook, stirring occasionally, until slightly transparent, about 4 minutes. Add all the mushrooms, pancetta, and thyme and stir to coat in the butter. Cook, stirring occasionally, until the mushrooms release their fluids and darken in color and the pancetta is crispy, about 10 minutes. Stir in the cream and sprinkle with the flour; allow to cook for 1 minute. Stir in the vegetable stock and simmer for 1 minute more. Remove from the heat. Dice the chicken and stir into the filling along with the garlic powder, onion powder, and salt to taste. Set aside.

Heat a large 12-inch nonstick skillet greased well with butter over high heat. Pour in about ½ cup batter, tilting the pan quickly as you pour to spread the batter in a thin even layer. Cook until golden on both sides, using your fingers to quickly pick up the crepe and flip it halfway through, 30 seconds to 2 minutes per side, depending on the heat of the pan and the thickness of the crepe.

Once cooked, remove the crepe and place one-fourth of the filling on one-fourth of the crepe. Fold the crepe in half over the filling and then fold the half over the filling to make a quarter circle. Serve immediately, then repeat with the remaining batter and filling three more times. You can also make all of the crepes, stack them, and then fill and serve.

Sage and Thyme Crepe Batter

1 cup all-purpose flour

½ teaspoon garlic powder

½ teaspoon onion powder

½ teaspoon rubbed dried sage

½ teaspoon dried thyme

½ teaspoon kosher salt

2 large eggs, beaten

½ cup milk

½ cup vegetable stock

¼ cup water

Chicken, Mushroom, and Pancetta Filling

4 tablespoons unsalted butter

½ pound chicken breast cutlets

1 shallot, finely diced

4 ounces oyster mushrooms, finely diced

2 ounces enoki mushrooms, coarsely chopped

2 ounces brown beech mushrooms, coarsely chopped

1 ounce diced pancetta

1 tablespoon minced fresh thyme leaves

2 teaspoons heavy cream

1 tablespoon all-purpose flour

2 tablespoons vegetable stock

1 teaspoon garlic powder

¾ teaspoon onion powder

Kosher salt to taste

Unsalted butter for greasing crepe pan

CHICKEN AND FETA FILO POCKETS

TIROPITA IS A TRADITIONAL SAVORY GREEK PASTRY full of cheese, herbs, spices, and, in this case, chicken. Ricotta and feta are mixed together with eggs, green onions, dill, and ground chicken that's been sautéed with fresh garlic. Dollops of the filling are wrapped up in buttered sheets of filo dough and baked until puffy, flaky, and golden. The filling becomes gooey and melted and the chicken provides a wonderful contrast in taste and texture to the tangy soft melted cheese. When working with filo, make sure to keep it covered with a kitchen towel once you've removed it from its package. It is very thin and will dry out very rapidly if left exposed. Work as quickly as possible to minimize the amount of time it is exposed to air. • makes about 24 pockets

1 tablespoon extra virgin olive oil

8 garlic cloves, minced

1 pound ground chicken

12 ounces feta cheese stored in brine, drained

12 ounces quality whole-milk ricotta cheese

2 large eggs, beaten

4 green onions, thinly sliced

3 tablespoons minced fresh dill

½ teaspoon kosher salt

¼ teaspoon freshly cracked black pepper

½ pound filo dough

8 tablespoons (1 stick) unsalted butter, melted

Heat the olive oil in a large frying pan over medium heat. Add the garlic and cook, stirring occasionally, until softened and fragrant, about 3 minutes. Add the ground chicken and cook, stirring occasionally and breaking the meat apart with the end of your spoon, until cooked through, 8 to 10 minutes. Set aside.

In a large mixing bowl, mix the feta and ricotta together. Add the eggs and stir until combined. Add the green onions, dill, salt, and black pepper and mix until thoroughly combined. Add the chicken mixture to the feta mixture and stir until combined to make the filling. Set aside.

Preheat the oven to 375°F. Grease a 12 by 17-inch baking sheet.

Take the filo dough out of the package and unroll it so it lays flat. Cover the filo with a dry kitchen towel and then a damp one to keep the sheets of dough from drying out while you're working.

Take a single sheet of the filo dough and brush it sparingly with melted butter. Now fold it in half lengthwise and brush the surface sparingly with butter again. Place 1 tablespoon of the filling in the bottom right corner of the strip. Fold the filo and filling over from the bottom right to the left to encase the filling and create a small triangle. Continue folding as you would fold a flag, folding the filling in the triangle up the sheet of dough. Seal the pocket by brushing the seam with butter, then place it seam-side down on the baking sheet. Brush the top with butter as well.

Repeat until all the filling has been used, making about 24 pockets. Bake until the filo dough is golden brown, 15 to 25 minutes. Let cool for 10 minutes before serving.

CHICKEN AND ROOT VEGETABLE GALETTE

Galette Dough

4 cups all-purpose flour

1 tablespoon kosher salt

2 teaspoons fresh marjoram, minced

2 teaspoons fresh thyme leaves

1 teaspoon garlic powder

1 teaspoon granulated sugar

½ teaspoon cumin

½ teaspoon freshly cracked black pepper

1¼ cups (2½ sticks) unsalted butter, frozen

⅔ to 1 cup ice water

Chicken and Root Vegetable Filling

1 pound boneless skinless chicken breast, cut into 1-inch cubes

1½ teaspoons kosher salt

½ teaspoon freshly cracked black pepper

4 tablespoons unsalted butter

2 tablespoons heavy cream

3 medium carrots, peeled and cut into ¼-inch-thick slices

1 turnip, peeled and cut into ¼-inch-thick slices

2 shallots, diced

4 garlic cloves, minced

1 tablespoon fresh thyme leaves

1½ teaspoons minced fresh marjoram

2 tablespoons all-purpose flour

1 large egg, beaten with 1 teaspoon water

WHEN WINTER COMES AROUND, nothing makes a more comforting pair than chicken and savory/sweet root vegetables like carrots and turnips. Here they are made into a galette, which is a flat open-faced pie with the crust's edges folded back slightly over the filling. As this cooks, the sugars in the vegetables break down and create a sweet and savory flavor combination that goes well with chicken and fresh herbs. Heaven in a crust! • serves 6

Preheat the oven to 375°F.

For the dough, in a large bowl, mix together the flour, salt, marjoram, thyme, garlic powder, sugar, cumin, and pepper. Grate the frozen butter over the bowl with the large hole setting of your grater, tossing the butter shards in the flour mixture to coat every 2 minutes or so to avoid ending up with one giant clump of butter.

Begin adding the ice water, 2 tablespoons at a time, while stirring gently. After about ⅔ cup of water, grab a handful of the dough and squeeze. If it generally sticks together when you let go, it is ready. If it completely crumbles apart, it needs a bit more water. Shape the dough into a ball, cover, and keep refrigerated until you're ready to roll it out, or up to 2 days in advance.

For the filling, toss the chicken with ½ teaspoon of the salt and the black pepper. Melt the butter in a large frying pan over medium heat. Add the chicken and cook, stirring occasionally, until golden and cooked through, about 6 minutes. Set aside.

Add the cream, carrots, turnip, shallots, garlic, thyme, and marjoram to the pan. Continue cooking over medium heat, stirring every minute, for 5 minutes. Add the flour by sprinkling it over the pan and stirring constantly until it is absorbed by the pan drippings and a thick sauce forms. Remove the pan from the heat. Add the chicken to the pan, and toss with the vegetables and remaining 1 teaspoon salt.

Roll the dough out on a lightly floured surface to a 14-inch round that is ¼ inch thick. Empty the filling into the center of the galette dough, spreading it out slightly so that it is circular and there is an approximate 2-inch border all around. Fold the excess dough over the filling, leaving the center area of the filling exposed and uncovered by the dough. Lightly brush the exposed dough with the egg wash. Bake for about 1 hour, until the edges are golden and the vegetables have softened. Cool for 15 minutes before serving.

Chicken, Mushroom & Cabbage Piroshki

Piroshki Dough

⅓ cup warm water

1 packet (2¼ teaspoons) active dry yeast

4 cups plus 2 tablespoons all-purpose flour

1 tablespoon light brown sugar

1 teaspoon kosher salt

1⅓ cups whole milk

1 large egg

3 tablespoons extra virgin olive oil

Chicken, Mushroom, and Cabbage Filling

2 tablespoons unsalted butter

1 large shallot, diced

8 ounces cabbage, thinly sliced (about 3 cups)

4 ounces white button mushrooms, diced

1 teaspoon dried savory

1 teaspoon kosher salt

½ teaspoon caraway seeds

¼ teaspoon freshly cracked black pepper

¼ teaspoon dried thyme

½ pound ground chicken

1 large egg, beaten with 1 teaspoon water

CARAWAY SEEDS PROVIDE THE PERFECT HERBAL and mildly bitter note for the filling in these piroshki, which are small stuffed Russian buns. Caraway enhances the slightly sour flavor of the cabbage, and sautéed mushrooms and ground chicken cut in with a warm and earthy richness that ties everything together. • makes about 20 piroshki

For the dough, in a small bowl, mix the warm water with the yeast and let sit for 10 minutes. In a large bowl, mix together the flour, brown sugar, and salt. Make a well in the center and add the milk, egg, olive oil, and yeast mixture. Stir until a thick dough forms.

Turn out the dough onto a lightly floured work surface. Knead until the dough is supple and smooth, about 10 minutes. Place in a lightly floured large bowl. Cover and let rise, at room temperature and out of direct sunlight, until doubled in size, about 2 hours.

Preheat the oven to 350°F. Line two baking sheets with parchment paper.

For the filling, melt the butter in a large Dutch oven over medium heat. Add the shallot and cook, stirring occasionally, until softened slightly, about 3 minutes. Add the cabbage, mushrooms, savory, salt, caraway, black pepper, and thyme and cook, stirring occasionally, until the cabbage softens, about 5 minutes. Add the ground chicken and cook, stirring occasionally, until cooked through, 8 to 10 minutes, breaking the chicken apart with the end of your stirring spoon as it cooks. Set aside to cool.

Grab a golf ball–sized piece of dough and roll out on a lightly floured surface to a 4-inch round that is about ⅛ inch thick. Add about 2 teaspoons of the filling to the center of the dough. Use a pastry brush to brush water along half of the edge of the round and fold it over, crimping the edges together with a fork to seal. Place on the baking sheet.

Repeat to make about 20 piroshki, leaving about 2 inches of space around each on the sheets. Lightly brush the piroshki with the egg wash using a pastry brush, and poke a fork into the top of each one to allow the steam to escape. Bake for about 25 minutes, until golden.

Burrata Chicken Pizza

This dish combines the best traditional pizza flavors with a few new savory additions. It begins with a quick homemade tomato sauce that can put any canned sauce to shame and creates the base flavor of the pizza. It is then topped with grated Parmesan, sliced burrata, a mozzarella-based cheese stuffed with cream, and Italian chicken sausage. Once baked, the whole thing is topped with fresh arugula. With your first bite you'll understand why this is such an incredible pizza. The gooey burrata gets tangled up in the fresh and crunchy arugula, and the sweet and tangy tomato sauce pairs perfectly with the bitter greens and creamy cheese, creating the ideal summer slice. • makes 2 pizzas, serving 4

For the pizza sauce, in a medium saucepan, bring the tomatoes, stock, tomato paste, garlic, sugar, salt, and pepper to a boil over medium-high heat. Reduce the heat to low and simmer, uncovered, stirring every 5 minutes, until the tomatoes nearly disintegrate, 20 to 30 minutes. Add the basil, stir, and cook for 3 more minutes. Set aside to cool.

For the crust, place a baking stone in the center rack of the oven and preheat the oven to 550°F. Prepare the pizza peel by generously coating it with semolina.

Take one of the dough balls and stretch it into a circle. Allow it to hang from your fists as you quickly rotate the circle, allowing gravity to stretch it out. Once it reaches about 12 inches in width, place it on the pizza peel.

For the toppings, heat the olive oil in a small frying pan over medium heat. Add the chicken sausage and cook, stirring occasionally, until cooked through. Let cool slightly and cut into ¼-inch-thick slices.

Spread half of the tomato sauce on the dough round, leaving a 1-inch border around the edge for the crust. Evenly distribute half of the burrata slices over the sauce. Sprinkle with half the Parmesan and arrange half of the sliced chicken sausage on top.

Open the oven and place the pizza peel ½ inch above the baking stone. Pull back very quickly to release the pizza from the peel so that it slides onto the stone. Bake for 10 to 15 minutes, until the pizza edges are golden and puffy and the center is cooked through. Remove and top with ½ cup of the arugula. Repeat with the remaining ingredients to make a second pizza. Serve immediately.

Pizza Sauce

2 plum tomatoes, diced

¼ cup chicken stock

3 tablespoons tomato paste

2 garlic cloves, minced

1 teaspoon granulated sugar

½ teaspoon kosher salt

½ teaspoon freshly cracked black pepper

2 teaspoons chopped fresh basil

Pizza Crust

Semolina flour, for pizza peel

Pizza Dough (page 194)

Toppings

1 teaspoon extra virgin olive oil

1 link Italian chicken sausage

2 ounces burrata, cut into ¼-inch-thick slices

1½ ounces Parmesan cheese, finely grated

1 cup arugula

Pizza Bianca
with Roasted Garlic and Chicken Sausage

2 heads garlic

2 tablespoons extra virgin olive oil

½ cup plus 6 tablespoons quality whole-milk ricotta cheese

2 tablespoons whole milk

¼ teaspoon kosher salt

¼ teaspoon freshly cracked black pepper

Semolina flour, for pizza peel

Pizza Dough (page 194)

2 thin slices prosciutto, torn into small pieces

¼ cup cooked Italian chicken sausage meat

THIS SIMPLE AND ELEGANT WHITE PIZZA PIE features roasted garlic–spiked ricotta, Italian sausage, and cured prosciutto. Roasted garlic is mashed into a paste and mixed with ricotta and a splash of milk to create a rich white sauce. Crumbled sausage is sprinkled on top, along with more roasted garlic and bits of salty prosciutto. Large dollops of the garlicky ricotta are splashed across the top. • makes 2 pizzas, serving 4

Preheat the oven to 400°F.

Cut the top fourth off the heads of garlic and discard the tops. Place each head in the center of a roughly 6 by 6-inch square of tinfoil. Drizzle the olive oil over the top of each garlic head and wrap the tinfoil up around each one like a parcel. Roast for 40 to 50 minutes, until aromatic and deeply golden. Use tongs to remove the garlic heads from the foil. Let cool completely. Take one garlic head and squeeze the softened roasted garlic paste out of the papery shell of the head. Discard the papery shell and reserve the roasted garlic paste. Peel the paper off the individual cloves of the remaining head. Set aside.

In a small bowl, mix together the roasted garlic paste, ricotta, milk, salt, and black pepper. Set aside.

Place a baking stone in the center rack of the oven and preheat the oven to 550°F. Prepare the pizza peel by generously coating it with semolina.

Take one of the dough balls and stretch it into a circle. Allow it to hang from your fists as you quickly rotate the circle, allowing gravity to stretch it out. Once it reaches 12 inches, place it on the pizza peel.

Spread about one-third of the ricotta mixture over the dough round, leaving a 1-inch border around the edge for the crust. Top with half of the prosciutto, chicken sausage, and roasted garlic cloves. Evenly distribute 3 individual tablespoon scoops of the ricotta on the pizza, leaving about 2 inches between each one.

Open the oven and place the pizza peel ½ inch above the baking stone. Pull back very quickly to release the pizza from the peel so that it slides onto the stone. Bake for 10 to 15 minutes, until the edges are golden and puffy and the center is cooked through. Repeat with the remaining ingredients to make a second pizza. Serve immediately.

WAFFLE PIZZA

Savory Waffle Batter

2 cups all-purpose flour

2 tablespoons light brown sugar

1 tablespoon baking powder

1 tablespoon minced fresh basil

¾ teaspoon kosher salt

½ teaspoon garlic powder

1½ cups whole milk

½ cup extra virgin olive oil

3 large eggs

Toppings

½ cup plus 2 tablespoons tomato pizza sauce (see page 193)

Scant 1 cup freshly grated Parmesan cheese (about 4 ounces)

10 ounces fresh mozzarella, cut into 15 thin slices

10 ounces Homemade Chicken and Apple Sausage links (page 130), or store-bought sausage, cooked and cut into 15 thin slices

Fresh basil leaves

BRACE YOURSELVES, BECAUSE THERE IS SUCH A THING as waffle pizza, and yes, it is incredibly delicious. The traditional waffle gets a savory twist with a touch of basil and garlic powder in the batter, and the cooked waffles are topped with a small dollop of tomato sauce, some cheese, and chicken sausage, then baked until the edges are crispy and the cheese is gooey. The key here is to use only a little tomato sauce on the waffle — too much and it will get soggy no matter how long you bake it. You just want a hint of that tomato flavor while allowing the waffle to stay nice and firm, perfect for slicing! • makes 5 waffle pizzas

---

For the waffles, in a medium bowl, mix the flour, brown sugar, baking powder, basil, salt, and garlic powder. Add the milk, olive oil, and eggs and whisk until just combined; it is okay if there are still a few lumps in the batter. Allow the batter to rest for 15 minutes.

Preheat the oven to 425°F.

Heat the waffle iron and cook 5 waffles according to manufacturer's directions.

For the toppings, spread 2 tablespoons of the pizza sauce on each waffle, then top each with 3 tablespoons Parmesan, 3 slices mozzarella, and 3 slices sausage.

Place the waffle pizzas on baking sheets and bake for about 10 minutes, until the cheese is melted and the tomato sauce darkens around the edges. Garnish with fresh basil and serve.

Pan-Fried Garlic Chicken Potstickers

I LOVE TO PAN-FRY POTSTICKERS because the thin gyoza wrappers crisp up perfectly in hot oil, creating a wonderfully crunchy meal. The filling is ground chicken sautéed with shallot, onions, garlic, mushrooms, and a mix of savory and sweet sauces. These are very easy to make and assemble, and the best part is that they freeze well, so you can make a large batch and freeze half of them in an airtight container for a rainy day. • makes about 24 potstickers

2 tablespoons extra virgin olive oil

4 garlic cloves, minced

1 shallot, minced

1 teaspoon minced fresh ginger

1 pound ground chicken

4 ounces cremini mushrooms, diced

1 tablespoon sesame oil

1 tablespoon oyster sauce

1 teaspoon fish sauce

1 teaspoon soy sauce

1 teaspoon dark sweet soy sauce

3 green onions, thinly sliced

12 ounces round gyoza wrappers

Warm water, for assembly

Canola oil, for frying

Heat the olive oil in a large skillet over medium heat. Add the garlic, shallot, and ginger and cook, stirring occasionally, until the shallot softens, about 5 minutes. Add the ground chicken, mushrooms, sesame oil, oyster sauce, fish sauce, soy sauce, and dark sweet soy sauce and cook, stirring to break up the chicken, until the chicken is cooked through and most of the liquid in the pan has evaporated. Add the green onions and cook, stirring occasionally, for 1 minute more. Remove from the heat.

On a clean work surface, place 1 teaspoon of the filling in the center of a gyoza wrapper. Dip your finger in warm water and trace it around the edge of the wrapper. Pleat one side of the circle, pressing it into the unpleated side of the wrapper to create a sealed pot sticker. Repeat until all of the wrappers and filling are used.

Heat ¼ inch of canola oil in a medium frying pan over medium heat. Flick a drop of water into the oil, if it sizzles it is ready for frying; if not, wait a few minutes and try again. Place the pot stickers in a single layer in the pan and fry until golden, turning to fry all three sides, about 2 minutes per side. Remove with tongs or a slotted spoon and drain on a plate lined with paper towels. Repeat with the remaining potstickers, adding more canola oil to the pan as needed between batches to maintain the ¼ inch depth. Serve immediately.

Noodles & Casseroles

Butternut Squash and Chicken Casserole *with Sage Béchamel*

Butternut Squash and Sweet Potatoes

½ butternut squash

2 medium sweet potatoes

½ teaspoon kosher salt

1 tablespoon extra virgin olive oil

Chicken

⅓ cup (⅔ stick) unsalted butter

1 pound ground chicken

2 garlic cloves, minced

1 medium yellow onion, diced

1 medium tomato, diced

¼ teaspoon rubbed dried sage

3 tablespoons tomato paste

3 tablespoons water

1 teaspoon kosher salt

½ teaspoon freshly cracked black pepper

½ teaspoon cinnamon

Sage Béchamel

⅓ cup (⅔ stick) unsalted butter

¼ cup cornstarch

3 cups whole milk

¾ teaspoon rubbed dried sage

¼ teaspoon cinnamon

¼ teaspoon nutmeg

¼ teaspoon kosher salt

3 egg yolks, beaten

LAYERS OF BUTTERNUT SQUASH AND SWEET POTATOES MELD together with spiced ground chicken in this savory and sweet casserole. The entire dish is topped with a sage-specked béchamel (white sauce) and baked until the vegetables soften and the béchamel becomes golden at the edges. It also includes a delicious sprinkling of Mizithra cheese, which is a hard cheese similar to Parmesan but made from sheep or goats' milk. The result is a meal with deep, rich flavors and a large helping of cold weather vegetables, making it a perfect dish for winter or fall. • serves 8

For the squash and sweet potatoes, peel the butternut squash and sweet potatoes and cut them into ¼-inch-thick slices. Sprinkle the salt on each side of the slices and set aside while you start the chicken.

For the chicken, melt the butter in a large frying pan over medium heat. Add the chicken and garlic and cook, stirring occasionally and breaking apart the meat with a large spoon or spatula, until the chicken is halfway cooked through, about 5 minutes. Add the onion, tomato, and sage and mix well. Continue to cook, stirring occasionally, until the chicken is cooked through, about 5 minutes. Add the tomato paste, water, salt, black pepper, and cinnamon. Mix well, reduce the heat, and simmer uncovered for about 20 minutes, until deep red in color.

Meanwhile, rinse the salt off of the sweet potato and squash slices and heat the olive oil in a wide and shallow pan. Cook each side of the sliced vegetables, frying for about 3 minutes per side until softened slightly. Set them aside on a plate lined with paper towels.

Preheat the oven to 350°F.

For the béchamel, melt the butter in a medium pan over low heat. Add the cornstarch and mix well until it forms a paste. Add the milk, ½ cup at a time, blending well after each addition. Stir in the sage, cinnamon, nutmeg, and salt and cook, uncovered and stirring every few minutes, for 10 minutes. Place the beaten egg yolks in a small bowl and add ½ cup of the milk mixture, whisking constantly. Add another ½ cup of the milk mixture to the bowl and mix well. Pour the egg yolk mixture back into the pan and whisk together until completely blended. Raise the heat to medium and continue cooking, stirring constantly, until the sauce thickens to a gravy-like consistency, 5 to 10 minutes. Set aside.

To assemble, grease a 9 by 13-inch casserole dish. Sprinkle about 1 tablespoon of the grated cheese in the dish as well as a pinch of black pepper and a pinch of sage. Create a single layer with about one-third of the butternut squash slices and sprinkle another tablespoon cheese and pinch of sage on top. Then create a single layer of one-third of the sweet potatoes and do the same with more cheese and sage. Repeat this process one more time so you have 2 alternating layers of butternut squash, cheese, sweet potatoes, and cheese. Pour the chicken mixture over the vegetable layers and create another layer of butternut squash and more cheese and sage, and another layer of sweet potatoes and more cheese and sage. Pour the béchamel over the top and sprinkle the remaining cheese on top. Bake for 45 minutes to 1 hour, until the top of the béchamel begins to brown. Let cool for 15 minutes before slicing and serving.

To Assemble the Casserole

½ cup grated Mizithra or Romano cheese

½ teaspoon freshly cracked black pepper

1 teaspoon rubbed dried sage

CHICKEN AND SEAFOOD PAELLA

1½ pounds chicken leg quarters (about 2), bone in and skin on

2 tablespoons extra virgin olive oil

2 tablespoons all-purpose flour

½ teaspoon kosher salt

2 ounces thinly sliced Spanish chorizo

1 medium yellow onion, diced

4 garlic cloves

2¾ cups chicken stock

1 cup uncooked paella rice

6 ounces cherry tomatoes, halved

1 teaspoon smoked paprika

½ teaspoon saffron threads

½ pound large shrimp, peeled and deveined

½ pound mussels

¼ pound littleneck clams

THE BEST PAELLA I EVER HAD WAS IN BARCELONA, and I've been chasing that dish ever since. I haven't found any here in the States that can rival it, but I was able to re-create it in all its glory with this recipe. There are a few keys to a good paella, and that's using quality paella rice and Spanish chorizo (cured not raw), and not skimping on the saffron. I know it is a very expensive spice, but if there is any time that it should be used with full force, it's when making paella. Tomatoes, garlic, onion, and chicken simmer away with the smoky rich chorizo sausage. The rice is added and right when it starts to soften, shrimp, mussels, and clams go in and the whole thing is popped in the oven, crisping up the exposed rice and making the interior rice wonderfully soft. The comforting flavors of the dish infuse into all the ingredients, making it one of the most deeply delicious rice dishes around. • serves 4

Cut each chicken quarter to separate the thigh from the drumstick, so that you have 2 whole drumsticks and 2 whole thighs. Heat the olive oil in a large paella pan or large frying pan over medium heat. In a small bowl, toss together the flour and salt. Coat the chicken with the flour mixture, add the chicken to the pan, and cook in the hot oil, stirring occasionally, until browned on both sides, 4 to 6 minutes per side. Remove the chicken and set aside.

Add the chorizo to the pan and cook, stirring occasionally, until it begins to release its fat, about 3 minutes. Add the onion and garlic and cook, stirring occasionally, until translucent, about 7 minutes.

Preheat the oven to 350°F.

Add the stock, rice, tomatoes, smoked paprika, and saffron threads and stir to combine. Nestle the chicken thighs and drumsticks back into the pot and simmer, uncovered, until the liquid in the pan thickens but the rice and chicken are not cooked through, about 10 minutes.

Stir in the shrimp, mussels, and clams. Transfer to the oven and roast for about 20 minutes, until the shrimp and chicken are cooked through. Cover with tinfoil. Let rest an additional 10 minutes before serving, discarding any mussels or clams that don't open.

SOURDOUGH CHICKEN CASSEROLE

I LOVE MAKING THIS CASSEROLE because it ends up providing toast, chicken, and a creamy and savory sauce to dip the toast in. It's a very easy and simple recipe, just make sure to get sourdough bread from the bakery section of your market, not the generic stuff from the bread aisle. Having a nice firm crust on the bread will help keep it from getting too soggy as it rests on top of the saucy lemon chicken and mushroom soup filling. • serves 4

Preheat the oven to 400°F.

In a medium bowl, whisk together the soup, olive oil, garlic, oregano, salt, and pepper until combined. Empty the mixture into a roughly 8 by 10-inch casserole dish. Add the chicken breasts and flip back and forth to coat in the mixture. Place the lemon wedges between the pieces of chicken and sprinkle the bread chunks on top. Sprinkle with an extra pinch of salt and pepper.

Cover with tinfoil and bake for about 50 minutes, until the bread is golden and crispy and the chicken is cooked through.

1 (10.5-ounce can) condensed cream of mushroom soup

½ cup extra virgin olive oil

2 garlic cloves, minced

3 tablespoons minced fresh oregano leaves

¾ teaspoon kosher salt

½ teaspoon freshly cracked black pepper

1½ pounds boneless skinless chicken breasts (about 3), cut in half

1 lemon, cut into sixths

½ loaf sourdough bread, torn into roughly 1-inch pieces

CHICKEN BIRYANI *with Saffron Quinoa*

Saffron Quinoa

2⅔ cups chicken stock

1 cinnamon stick

⅛ teaspoon saffron

1½ cups quinoa

Chicken Biryani

3 tablespoons unsalted butter

1 tablespoon extra virgin olive oil

4 small chicken leg quarters (about 2¼ pounds), bone in and skin on

1½ teaspoons kosher salt

1 large onion, chopped

2 bay leaves

2 cardamom pods

1 cinnamon stick

2 garlic cloves, minced

1 tablespoon grated fresh ginger

1½ teaspoons curry powder

1½ teaspoons ground turmeric

½ to ¼ teaspoon chili powder

1 cup plain full-fat yogurt

⅔ cup chicken stock

½ cup golden raisins

¼ cup chopped fresh cilantro

THIS RICHLY SPICED STEW, BIRYANI, HAS INCREDIBLE FLAVOR and texture. Traditionally, it is made with basmati rice and contains many spices, including cardamom, cinnamon, and bay leaves. Here it is prepared with the same traditional seasonings, but with quinoa instead of rice, making for a healthier and more protein-rich meal. Most of the preparation is done on the stovetop, but then you transfer the pot to the oven to bake until the flavors permeate the entire dish and the quinoa develops a lovely golden crust on top, while the layer underneath stays hot and fluffy. This, along with the incredible aroma that fills your kitchen as the biryani bakes, makes it one of my go-to dinners. • serves 4

For the saffron quinoa, bring the stock with the cinnamon stick and saffron to a boil in a medium saucepan over medium heat. Add the quinoa, reduce the heat to low, and cover. Cook, stirring every 5 minutes, for 15 minutes, until the quinoa has absorbed the liquid. Let stand for 5 minutes. Fluff the quinoa lightly with a fork and set aside.

Preheat the oven to 375°F.

For the chicken biryani, melt the butter with the olive oil in a large Dutch oven over medium heat. Sprinkle the chicken legs with ½ teaspoon of the salt, add to the Dutch oven, and cook until lightly browned all over, about 10 minutes per side. Remove the chicken pieces from the Dutch oven and set them aside, leaving the fat in the pan.

Add the onion, bay leaves, cardamom pods, cinnamon stick, and remaining 1 teaspoon salt and cook, stirring, until the onion is translucent and gold around the edges, about 10 minutes. Add the garlic, ginger, curry powder, turmeric, and chili powder and cook, stirring once a minute, for 3 minutes. Let cool for 5 minutes. Whisk in the yogurt and stock. Return to low heat and cook for 3 minutes. Stir in the raisins and cilantro. Add the chicken and coat it in the sauce. Add the quinoa and stir so that it is evenly distributed throughout the dish.

Cover the pot and bake in the oven for 15 minutes. Uncover and bake for 40 minutes longer, until the exposed quinoa is very lightly crisp. Discard the bay leaves and serve immediately.

Pesto-Penne Chicken Bake

HOMEMADE PESTO FLAVORS PENNE AND CHICKEN for an incredibly refreshing and intensely flavorful casserole. This pesto's key ingredient is pistachios, which intensifies the green hue of the pesto and adds a savory sweet element. You can use nearly any kind of pasta if you happen to have another type on hand. I've prepared the casserole with elbow macaroni and bow tie pasta, and it tastes just as delicious. • serves 6

For the pesto, blend the pine nuts, walnuts, and pistachios in a food processor until finely chopped, about 20 seconds. Add the basil and garlic and blend until smooth, about 30 seconds. While the food processor is running, slowly pour the olive oil into the feed tube. Add the Parmesan, salt, and black pepper and blend until completely smooth. Empty into a bowl and cover with plastic wrap, pressing the plastic wrap onto the top of the pesto. Makes about 3 cups. Place in the refrigerator for up to 1 week.

For the casserole, heat 2 tablespoons of the olive oil in a medium frying pan. Coat the chicken breasts with the salt and pepper and add it to the pan. Cook until lightly golden on both sides and completely cooked through, about 30 minutes. Set aside to cool. Cut the chicken into 1-inch-thick strips.

Preheat the oven to 375°F.

Prepare the penne according to the package directions, until al dente. Drain and rinse with cold water to prevent the pasta from continuing to cook. Toss with the remaining 1 tablespoon olive oil and set aside.

In a large bowl, mix 2 cups of the pesto, the ricotta, and crème fraîche until smooth. Add the chicken and penne and toss to coat. Empty the mixture into a large casserole dish and sprinkle the Parmesan on top. Bake for about 30 minutes, until the tips of the penne are golden brown. Serve immediately.

Pesto

⅓ cup pine nuts

⅓ cup walnuts

¼ cup shelled pistachios

4½ cups packed fresh basil leaves

8 garlic cloves, minced

1 cup plus 2 tablespoons extra virgin olive oil

1 cup plus 2 tablespoons freshly grated Parmesan cheese

¾ teaspoon kosher salt

¾ teaspoon freshly cracked black pepper

Penne-Chicken Casserole

3 tablespoons extra virgin olive oil

1 pound boneless skinless chicken breasts (about 2)

½ teaspoon kosher salt

½ teaspoon freshly cracked black pepper

12 ounces dry penne pasta

½ cup quality whole-milk ricotta cheese

¼ cup crème fraîche or sour cream

3 tablespoons freshly grated Parmesan cheese

Sweet Potato–Chicken Casserole

1½ teaspoons kosher salt

1 teaspoon mustard powder

1 teaspoon rubbed dried sage

1 teaspoon dried savory

½ teaspoon sweet Hungarian paprika

4 chicken thighs (about 2 pounds), bone in and skin on

½ cup plus 2 tablespoons extra virgin olive oil

1 cup chicken stock

1 cup water

3 pounds sweet potatoes, peeled and cut into 2-inch cubes

1 cup raw walnuts

½ cup chopped pitted dates

THIS SWEET AND SALTY DISH COMBINES MY FAVORITE MEAT with my favorite root vegetable. Sweet potatoes are tossed in olive oil and spices, then roasted with chicken thighs, dates, and walnuts. The chicken roasts to golden brown and the edges of the potatoes become nice and crisp. It's what I'd call a crowd pleaser. • serves 4

———————————————

Preheat the oven to 400°F.

In a small bowl, combine the salt, mustard powder, sage, savory, and paprika. Rub the chicken with 2 tablespoons of the olive oil and sprinkle each thigh with ½ teaspoon of the spice mixture. Set aside.

Whisk the remaining spice mixture with the remaining ½ cup olive oil, the stock, and water. Empty into a roughly 9 by 13-inch casserole dish and add the sweet potatoes, walnuts, and dates. Toss to coat. Arrange the chicken in the pan with the potatoes around it. Roast for about 1 hour, until the potatoes are tender when poked with a fork and the chicken is cooked through. Serve.

CHICKEN AND MUSHROOM LASAGNA
with Brown Butter–Garlic Béchamel

THE EARTHY FLAVORS OF MUSHROOMS PAIR PERFECTLY with subtle chicken in this hearty lasagna. You won't find tomato sauce here, but instead a glorious helping of cheese. That and the brown butter–garlic béchamel makes this a lasagna that you won't be able to forget. • serves 8

Melt 6 tablespoons of the butter in a large frying pan over medium heat. Add all the mushrooms and cook, stirring occasionally, until they have darkened in color and released some of their moisture, about 8 minutes. Remove from the pan with a slotted spoon and set aside. Place the chicken, thyme, and ½ teaspoon of the salt in the same pan and cook, stirring occasionally, until cooked through, breaking the chicken apart with the end of your spoon as it cooks. Remove with a slotted spoon and set aside.

Add the remaining 3 tablespoons butter to the pan and let melt completely. Add the garlic and reduce the heat to low. Allow the butter to deepen in color, stirring about every 3 minutes, until it turns lightly golden and smells nutty and intensely of garlic, 10 to 15 minutes. Whisk in the flour until a thick paste forms, about 30 seconds. Add the milk and remaining ½ teaspoon salt and whisk constantly until a thick béchamel forms. Bring to a simmer and cook for 5 minutes. Crumble the chèvre over the top and stir until smooth. Set aside.

Preheat the oven to 375°F. Whisk the ricotta with the eggs and rosemary until smooth. Set aside.

Bring a large pot of water to a boil. Add the lasagna noodles and boil until softened slightly, about 3 minutes. Remove with tongs and pat dry.

Spread one-fifth of the béchamel in a 9 by 13-inch casserole dish that is at least 3 inches deep. Cover with an even layer of the lasagna noodles (about 3), then one-fourth of the mushrooms and one-fourth of the chicken. Sprinkle with ¼ cup of the Parmesan, then cover with one-fourth of the ricotta mixture and top with generous ⅓ cup of the Gouda and a pinch of the black pepper. Repeat this process 3 times so you have 4 layers of these ingredients. Top with the remaining béchamel and sprinkle with the remaining ¼ cup Parmesan.

Bake for 35 to 40 minutes, until the edges are bubbling and the top has some golden spots. Let cool for 20 minutes before slicing and serving.

9 tablespoons unsalted butter

10 ounces cremini mushrooms, thickly sliced

8 ounces white button mushrooms, thickly sliced

2 ounces chanterelle mushrooms, thickly sliced

8 ounces shiitake mushrooms, thickly sliced

1 pound ground chicken

2 tablespoons fresh thyme leaves

1 teaspoon kosher salt

6 garlic cloves, minced

⅓ cup all-purpose flour

2½ cups whole milk

4 ounces chèvre, crumbled

30 ounces quality fresh whole milk ricotta cheese

2 large eggs, beaten

1 tablespoon minced fresh rosemary leaves

8 ounces lasagna noodles

1¼ cups grated Parmesan cheese (about 5 ounces)

1½ cups grated aged Gouda cheese (about 6 ounces)

¼ teaspoon freshly cracked black pepper

Chicken Stuffed Pumpkin

This sumptuous autumn dish is as delicious as it is beautiful. A sweet and savory rice pudding of chicken, fruit, cream, herbs, and spices simmers inside a small pumpkin as it roasts in the oven. The essence of the pumpkin seeps into the rich rice mixture, and the flavors of the fruits and spices infuse into the flesh of the pumpkin, creating the tastiest symbiotic relationship ever. The best part is that you can serve the rice right out of the pumpkin and eat the bowl, too! • serves 2

Carve out the cap of the pumpkin, leaving a few inches of space around the stem. Reserve the cap. Scoop out the pulp and seeds and discard. Rinse out the pumpkin and pat dry with paper towels. Brush the warm honey on the outside of the pumpkin and pat the brown sugar onto it until coated. Set aside.

In a medium pot, bring 2 cups of the stock and the water to a boil and add the rice. Stir, reduce the heat to low, and simmer for 20 minutes, covered. Drain; the rice should not be fully cooked at this point.

Preheat the oven to 325°F. Line a baking sheet with parchment paper.

In a medium frying pan, heat the olive oil over medium heat. Add the chicken and onion and cook until the chicken is nearly, but not completely, cooked through, 6 to 8 minutes, breaking apart the ground chicken pieces with the end of your spoon as it cooks. Set aside.

In a large bowl, toss together the rice, chicken and onion, pears, raisins, melted butter, cream, palm sugar, salt, cinnamon, nutmeg, and allspice until the ingredients are evenly distributed.

Gently scoop the rice mixture into the hollowed-out pumpkin until it is full, taking care not to pack in the stuffing. Pour the remaining ¼ cup stock over the top of the rice mixture and place the cap back on the pumpkin. Place the pumpkin on the baking sheet and bake for 1½ to 2 hours, until the rice is cooked all the way through and the pumpkin's skin turns dark orange. Let cool for 20 minutes before serving.

1 small sugar pumpkin (2 to 3 pounds)

3 tablespoons honey, warm

¼ cup dark brown sugar

2¼ cups chicken stock

½ cup water

1½ cups uncooked white rice

1 tablespoon extra virgin olive oil

1 pound ground chicken

1 cup chopped yellow onion

2 large ripe pears, peeled, cored, and chopped

¼ cup golden raisins

4 tablespoons unsalted butter, melted

2 tablespoons heavy cream

2 tablespoons palm or coconut sugar

½ teaspoon kosher salt

½ teaspoon cinnamon

¼ teaspoon nutmeg

¼ teaspoon allspice

Dijon-Chicken Macaroni and Cheese
with Caramelized Onion

Caramelized Onion

2 tablespoons unsalted butter

1 tablespoon extra virgin
olive oil

1 yellow onion

1 teaspoon light brown sugar

Chicken

4 small drumsticks (about
1 pound)

4 small chicken thighs (about
1¾ pounds), bone in and
skin on

2 teaspoons kosher salt

1 teaspoon freshly cracked black
pepper

2 tablespoons unsalted butter

2 tablespoons extra virgin
olive oil

Macaroni and Cheese

1 pound elbow pasta

1 tablespoon extra virgin
olive oil

2¼ cups whole milk

3 tablespoons unsalted butter

⅓ cup all-purpose flour

1 pound sharp white cheddar
cheese, grated

5 ounces Gruyère cheese, grated

½ cup grainy Dijon mustard

1½ teaspoons freshly cracked
black pepper

½ cup panko bread crumbs

I LOVE SLATHERING MY GRILLED CHEESE SANDWICHES with grainy Dijon mustard, so I decided to combine the two in a breaded mac and cheese. I use good ol' white cheddar and Gruyère because they're my favorites to pair with Dijon, but you could sub in a similar cheese like Swiss or Gouda if you happen to have it on hand. I also toss in some caramelized onion, and (of course) chicken—in this case bone-in thighs and drumsticks. Once everything is baked together with elbow pasta in the thick, cheesy sauce, you'll have my favorite macaroni and cheese of all time. • serves 8

For the caramelized onion, melt the butter with the olive oil in a large Dutch oven over medium heat. Add the onion and brown sugar and reduce the heat to medium low. Cook, stirring every 5 minutes, until golden brown and fragrant, about 30 minutes. Remove the onion from the pot and set aside.

Preheat the oven to 375°F.

For the chicken, coat the drumsticks and thighs with the salt and pepper. Melt the butter with the olive oil in the Dutch oven over medium-high heat. Add the chicken and cook until browned on both sides; the pieces do not need to be completely cooked through. Remove from the pot and set aside.

For the macaroni and cheese, prepare the pasta according to the package directions, until al dente. Rinse with cold water to prevent overcooking, drain, and toss with the olive oil. Set aside.

Heat the milk in a medium saucepan over medium-low heat, stirring every 3 minutes, until hot but not boiling. Meanwhile, melt the butter in the Dutch oven over medium heat. Whisk in the flour until a thick paste forms and continue cooking and stirring for 30 seconds. Whisk the hot milk into the butter mixture and cook for 2 more minutes, still whisking constantly. Add the cheddar, Gruyère, mustard, and 1 teaspoon of the black pepper and stir until the cheese has melted.

In a large bowl, toss the cheese sauce with the onion, pasta, and chicken. Empty into a large casserole dish and top with the panko crumbs and remaining ½ teaspoon black pepper. Bake for 30 to 40 minutes, until the chicken is cooked through, the top is golden, and the cheese sauce is bubbly. Serve immediately.

Spinach, Chicken, Manchego, and Feta Tortellini

I LOVE MAKING HOMEMADE PASTA BECAUSE IT'S SO EASY and rewarding. Fresh pasta is incredibly delicious and affordable, and it also allows you to customize a filling when you make stuffed pasta like these little guys. Spinach, chicken, Manchego cheese, and feta combine to create a savory filling for pasta that is creamy, refreshing, and comforting. I highly recommend pairing this with either a garlic and olive oil–based sauce, or a pesto-based one. • serves 6

For the filling, heat the olive oil in a medium frying pan over medium-high heat. Add the shallot and garlic and cook, stirring occasionally, until lightly transparent, about 5 minutes. Add the ground chicken and cook, stirring occasionally and breaking apart the chicken with the end of your spoon as it cooks, until nearly cooked through, about 6 minutes. Add the spinach, stir to combine, and cook until it is wilted and has shrunk significantly and the chicken is completely cooked, about 5 minutes. Remove from the heat and drain excess liquid from the pan. Crumble the feta cheese over the filling and stir it in along with the Manchego.

To make the tortellini, lightly flour a baking sheet and set it aside. Fill a small bowl with warm water and keep it near the work area. Divide the dough in half, set aside one half, and cover it with a damp kitchen towel. Run the uncovered half through a pasta roller at progressively thinner settings to achieve a paper-thin sheet of dough, or roll out the dough by hand on a well-floured surface as thin as you can manage. Use a 3-inch round cookie cutter to cut out the tortellini shapes. Place 1 teaspoon of the filling in the center of one circle. Dip your finger in the warm water and run it around the edge of the circle. Fold the dough over the filling to form a half-circle, pressing the edges to seal. Bring the two corners together over the filling and press the edges together between your index finger and thumb. Continue making tortellini, placing them on the floured baking sheet as you complete them. Repeat with the remaining dough and filling.

To cook the tortellini, bring a large pot of water to a boil with a pinch of salt. Use a slotted spoon to add the tortellini to the pot, a few at a time, and cook, stirring every minute to keep the tortellini from sticking to each other and the bottom of the pan, until the tortellini have floated to the surface, about 6 minutes. Drain, top with your desired sauce, and serve.

2 tablespoons extra virgin olive oil

1 shallot, diced

3 garlic cloves, minced

1 pound ground chicken

¾ cup minced spinach

⅓ cup feta cheese stored in brine, drained

⅓ cup finely grated Manchego cheese

Pasta Dough (page 218)

If you're not cooking the tortellini immediately, you can place the baking sheet in the freezer for 2 hours, and then transfer the frozen individual tortellini into an air-tight freezer-safe container and return to the freezer. Use within 4 months.

CHICKEN FETTUCCINE ALFREDO

2 pounds chicken thighs, bone in and skin on

1 tablespoon extra virgin olive oil

¾ teaspoon kosher salt

1¼ teaspoons freshly cracked black pepper

8 tablespoons (1 stick) unsalted butter

2 garlic cloves, minced

1 cup crème fraîche

½ cup milk

6 ounces pecorino Romano cheese, freshly grated

6 ounces Parmesan cheese, freshly grated

6 ounces Asiago cheese, freshly grated

1 pound dry fettuccine pasta

1 tablespoon fresh basil leaves, for garnish (optional)

ALFREDO IS ONE OF THE SIMPLEST AND RICHEST PASTA SAUCES out there; this version brings the flavors of the sauce up a notch by combining pecorino Romano, Parmesan, and Asiago cheese. To create a truly excellent Alfredo sauce it is vital to use quality cheese. Bypass the pre-shredded stuff in a plastic tub that's sitting at room temperature and only purchase chilled cheese that is in a solid block so you can freshly grate it yourself. Trust me, once you've tasted the nutty, creamy flavors of a true unadulterated Alfredo sauce, you'll be very happy you did. • serves 4

Preheat the oven to 350°F.

Rub the chicken with the olive oil, salt, and ½ teaspoon of the black pepper. Place on a baking sheet and roast for about 1 hour, until the skin is golden and crisp and the juices run clear. Set aside to cool, then remove the meat from the bones and cut it into roughly 2-inch by 1-inch strips.

Melt the butter with the garlic in a medium saucepan over low heat. Add the crème fraîche, milk, Romano, Parmesan, Asiago, and remaining ¾ teaspoon black pepper and continue cooking, stirring constantly, until the cheese has melted and the sauce is smooth. Set aside.

Cook the fettuccine noodles according to package directions until al dente. Top with the Alfredo sauce and chicken; garnish with basil leaves, if desired; and serve immediately.

Chicken Pad See Ew

If you couldn't already tell from the abundance of Thai-inspired dishes in this book, I am slightly obsessed with Thai flavors (my husband and I may have planned our entire honeymoon in Thailand solely on eating our way through the country), and this dish is what started it all. I first had it my freshman year of college and nearly gasped at how good it was. Sweet and salty in a way that Western cuisines cannot replicate, the heart of pad see ew lies in the use of dark sweet soy sauce, a fermented soy sauce that is turned into an almost black syrup with an intensely sweet and fermented flavor. This is combined with oyster sauce, regular soy sauce, brown sugar, garlic, and vinegar to create the incredible savory, tangy, and sweet gravy-like sauce that coats the rice noodles, chicken, and broccoli. The result is a traditional Thai dish that's unparalleled in its richness of flavor. • serves 2

2 tablespoons oyster sauce

2 teaspoons soy sauce

2 teaspoons light brown sugar

2 teaspoons white vinegar

3 garlic cloves, minced

½ pound boneless skinless chicken breast, cut into ½-inch-thick slices

1 (8-ounce) package dried wide rice noodles

¼ cup vegetable oil

1 large egg, beaten

1¼ cups loosely packed broccoli florets

2 tablespoons plus 1 teaspoon sweet dark soy sauce

In a small bowl, mix together the oyster sauce, soy sauce, brown sugar, vinegar, and garlic until well blended. Set aside.

Fill a medium saucepan two-thirds full with water and bring to a simmer over medium-high heat. Add the sliced chicken breast and simmer until almost cooked through, 4 to 5 minutes. Drain and set aside.

Fill another medium saucepan two-thirds full with water and bring to a simmer over medium-high heat. Add the rice noodles and simmer, stirring every minute, until they just begin to soften and become flexible, 4 to 7 minutes. Drain and rinse with cold water. Set aside.

The next steps need to happen very quickly so it is important that all your remaining ingredients are measured out before you start this process. Heat the oil in a large wok over high heat. Add the egg and quickly scramble it in the hot oil with the end of a large metal spoon. Add the rice noodles and the oyster sauce mixture and stir until the noodles are coated in the sauce. Let them sit in the sauce for 30 seconds, stir, and then let them sit for another 30 seconds. Add the chicken, broccoli, and dark sweet soy sauce and cook, stirring every 30 seconds, until the chicken is cooked through, about 3 minutes. Serve immediately.

Sandwiches, Burgers & Wraps

ROASTED GARLIC–CHICKEN SANDWICHES
with Arugula

I'M A BIG FAN OF GARLIC, but my absolute favorite way to enjoy it is roasted. It's incredibly easy to make (just wrap a head of garlic in tinfoil and bake) and adds a depth of flavor to dishes that is sometimes indescribable —but as soon as you say "roasted garlic" the beneficiary of the dish nods knowingly and happily. I incorporate some fresh arugula into these garlicky chicken sandwiches to enhance the crunch of the breaded chicken and add a bit of brightness to the sandwich. • serves 4

Preheat the oven to 375°F.

Cut the top quarter off the heads of garlic and discard. Place each garlic head in the center of a roughly 6 by 6-inch square of tinfoil, with the cut side facing up. Drizzle with the olive oil. Wrap the tinfoil around each head and twist slightly at the top to make a little airtight bundle.

In a medium bowl, mix together the bread crumbs, salt, black pepper, and garlic powder. Lay each of the chicken breasts flat between 2 sheets of plastic wrap. Use a meat tenderizing mallet to flatten the chicken slightly so it is roughly 1 inch thick throughout the breast. Dip each of the breasts in the egg and then dredge in the bread crumb mixture to coat. Place on a baking sheet along with the foil-wrapped garlic. Roast for about 45 minutes, until the chicken is cooked through and the garlic is deeply golden and aromatic.

Unwrap the garlic and allow it to cool before removing it from the foil. Turn the garlic upside down and use your hands to squeeze the roasted garlic out of the skins and into a small flat-bottomed bowl. Add the mayonnaise and black pepper and use a fork to mash the garlic into the mayonnaise until thoroughly combined.

Spread about 1 heaping tablespoon of the garlic mayo onto one side of each of the two bread slices. Place a chicken breast on one of the slices and top with ¼ cup of the arugula. Place the other slice of bread on top. Repeat with the remaining ingredients until you have 4 complete sandwiches. Serve immediately.

4 heads garlic

1 tablespoon extra virgin olive oil

1 cup dried bread crumbs

1 teaspoon kosher salt

1 teaspoon freshly cracked black pepper

1 teaspoon garlic powder

2 boneless skinless chicken breasts (about 1 pound), cut in half widthwise

1 large egg, beaten

8 teaspoons mayonnaise

¼ teaspoon freshly cracked black pepper

8 slices rosemary bread

1 cup arugula

CHICKEN BANH MI *with Quick-Pickled Carrots*

Quick-Pickled Carrots

2 medium carrots, peeled

¼ cup rice vinegar

1 tablespoon water

½ teaspoon grated fresh ginger

Soy-Roasted Chicken

3 tablespoons soy sauce

1 tablespoon ponzu

1 tablespoon sesame oil

1 teaspoon mirin

1 teaspoon rice vinegar

1¾ pounds chicken drumsticks

½ teaspoon garlic powder

½ teaspoon sesame seeds

¼ teaspoon ground dried ginger

Banh Mi

½ pound salt pork belly

1 tablespoon canola oil

4 tablespoons minced fresh cilantro

4 small baguettes; or 1 standard baguette, cut into 4 segments

BANH MI SANDWICHES ARE PROBABLY THE MOST REFRESHING around. They're a traditional Vietnamese snack, created during France's colonization of the country, that marries freshly baked baguettes with pickled root vegetables, cilantro, fried pork belly, and some kind of meat —in this case, soy-roasted chicken. The quick-pickled carrots add a crunch and sweet-and-sour tang to the sandwich, which helps cut through the rich pork belly and savory dark meat, and the cilantro adds a revitalizing freshness to the whole thing. I used heirloom carrot varieties here, but plain old orange carrots work just fine. The make-or-break aspect of this sandwich, however, is the baguette. Try to get ones from your bakery that have been made that same day; a fluffy baguette makes all the difference! • serves 4

For the quick-pickled carrots, use a mandoline or vegetable peeler to cut the carrots into long thin slices. Place in a small bowl. In a small saucepan, bring the vinegar, water, and ginger to a boil. Pour the hot vinegar mixture over the carrots and toss to coat. Let cool to room temperature before covering with plastic wrap and refrigerating for at least 1 hour. It will keep up to 1 week in a refrigerated airtight container.

For the chicken, preheat the oven to 350°F.

In a medium bowl, whisk together the soy sauce, ponzu, sesame oil, mirin, and rice vinegar. Toss the drumsticks with the sauce and place on a baking sheet. In a small bowl, whisk together the garlic powder, sesame seeds, and dried ginger. Sprinkle the drumsticks with the seasonings. Bake for about 1 hour, until the skin is crisp and the chicken is cooked through. Let cool. Remove the meat from the bones and set aside.

For the banh mi, cut the pork belly into 8 roughly 2 by 4-inch rectangles that are ½ inch thick. Heat the canola oil in a small frying pan over medium-high heat. Pan-fry the pork belly slices until golden and crispy on both sides, about 5 minutes. Transfer to a plate lined with paper towels to drain.

Evenly distribute the chicken, pickled carrots, pork belly, and cilantro between the 4 baguettes. Serve immediately.

Parmesan Chicken Breakfast Sandwiches

THERE'S AN INTERPLAY BETWEEN SALTY, crunchy Parmesan chicken fillets and mildly anise-like tarragon that is uniquely mouthwatering. When you bring a fried egg and chive crème fraîche into the mix, you end up with a breakfast sandwich that is unparalleled in its deliciousness. It is key to use fresh rosemary bread for this recipe: Almost every major grocery store's bakery makes a rosemary loaf, and the fluffy herbal bread provides the perfect complement to the intensely savory fillings. • serves 4

Preheat the oven to 350°F. Line a baking sheet with tinfoil.

Mix together the bread crumbs, Parmesan, 1 teaspoon of the salt, and ½ teaspoon of the black pepper in a shallow bowl. Rub the chicken with 2 tablespoons of the olive oil and dredge in the bread crumb mixture to coat. Place on the baking sheet and roast for about 30 minutes, until the chicken is cooked through. Set aside.

In a small bowl, whisk together the crème fraîche, chives, remaining ¼ teaspoon salt, and remaining ¼ teaspoon black pepper and set aside.

Spread 1 teaspoon of the butter on each slice of bread and toast on a skillet over medium high heat until golden on each side. Place each chicken cutlet on a slice of bread.

Heat the remaining 2 tablespoons olive oil in a large frying pan over low heat. Once a drop of water flicked into the pan sizzles slightly, the oil is ready. Add the eggs to the pan, spacing them out as evenly as possible. Cover and cook until the egg whites have nearly solidified and the yolks are still wiggly, about 5 minutes depending on the heat intensity.

Place each egg on top of a chicken cutlet. Top with several generous tablespoonfuls of the chive crème fraîche and 1 tablespoon of the tarragon. Place the remaining bread slices on each sandwich and serve immediately.

2 cups panko bread crumbs

1⅓ cups finely grated Parmesan cheese

1¼ teaspoons kosher salt

¾ teaspoon freshly cracked black pepper

4 boneless skinless chicken breast cutlets

4 tablespoons extra virgin olive oil

½ cup crème fraîche or sour cream

3 tablespoons finely chopped fresh chives

8 teaspoons unsalted butter, at room temperature

8 slices rosemary bread

4 large eggs

¼ cup chopped fresh tarragon leaves

Fried Chicken and Maple–Pork Belly Waffle Sandwiches

Maple–Pork Belly Waffle Batter

1 teaspoon vegetable oil

2 ounces salt cured pork belly, diced

1½ cups all-purpose flour

¾ cup cornmeal

¼ cup pure maple sugar

3 tablespoons light brown sugar

1 tablespoon baking powder

1 teaspoon kosher salt

3 large eggs

1½ cups whole milk

¼ cup extra virgin olive oil

¼ cup pure maple syrup

Fried Chicken

3 boneless skinless chicken breasts (about 1½ pounds)

½ cup cornmeal

¼ cup all-purpose flour

¼ cup panko bread crumbs

2 tablespoons light brown sugar

1 large egg, beaten

Canola oil, for frying

3 tablespoons unsalted butter, softened

1 tablespoon pure maple sugar

¾ teaspoon kosher salt

THE BATTER FOR THESE SAVORY WAFFLES has a little extra something, and that something is pan-fried pork belly bits. They also have a bit of cornmeal to make a waffle that is slightly reminiscent of cornbread. Pretty much anything would taste good sandwiched between two of these waffles, but when you make it fried breaded chicken breasts with maple sugar, you have a pretty exceptional sandwich on your hands. • serves 3

———————————————

Lay each chicken breast flat between two sheets of plastic wrap on a clean work surface. Use a meat mallet to hammer the meat and flatten it so that it is roughly ¾-inch thick all around. Remove the plastic wrap and cover and refrigerate the chicken.

For the waffle batter, heat the vegetable oil in a medium frying pan over medium heat. Add the pork belly and cook, stirring occasionally, until cooked through and crisp around the edges, 4 to 5 minutes. Set aside.

In a medium bowl, whisk together the flour, cornmeal, maple sugar, brown sugar, baking powder, and salt. In another medium bowl, whisk together the eggs, milk, olive oil, and maple syrup until smooth. Add the dry ingredients to the milk mixture and stir until just combined. Stir in the diced pork belly. Allow the batter to rest for 15 minutes.

Heat a waffle iron and cook 6 waffles per the manufacturer's directions.

For the fried chicken, mix the cornmeal, flour, bread crumbs, and brown sugar together in a shallow medium bowl. Place the beaten egg in a second bowl. Add 3 inches canola oil to a medium saucepan and heat to 350°F over medium-high heat. Pat each chicken breast dry. Dip in the egg to moisten, then dredge in the flour mixture to coat. Place in the oil and fry, turning once, until golden brown and cooked through, about 7 minutes per side. Transfer to a plate lined with paper towels to drain.

To assemble the sandwiches, in a small bowl, mix together the butter, maple sugar, and salt until smooth. Smear the butter on one side of each waffle. Place a chicken breast on the buttered side of 3 waffles and place another waffle on top of each, buttered side facing down. Repeat with the remaining ingredients to make 3 waffle sandwiches and serve immediately.

CHICKEN SOUVLAKI SANDWICHES
with Homemade Tzatziki

FOR ME, THIS IS WHAT SUMMER TASTES LIKE: Char-grilled marinated chicken covered with a cool refreshing cucumber yogurt sauce, crisp veggies, and crumbled feta cheese, all wrapped up in a toasted fluffy pita bread. Using quality pita bread is very important here, do not use the 'pockets' that have horizontal holes pre-cut into them as these are very dry and crumbly. You want whole, thick, soft, and fluffy pitas that will hold up to heaps of delicious toppings. It's at once both comforting and refreshing, offering a respite from the heat with the creamy yogurt and cucumber tzatziki, but reminding you of how much you love it with every bite of the hot and succulent bird. • serves 6

For the tzatziki, cut the cucumbers in half lengthwise. Use a small spoon to scoop out and discard the soft seed pulp in the center. Grate the cucumbers on the large hole setting of your grater, about ¼-inch in diameter. Place the cucumber in a sieve placed over a bowl and press on the cucumbers, expressing them of their juice. Discard the liquid.

Add the yogurt to the cucumber in the large bowl, along with the garlic, olive oil, vinegar, salt, and pepper. Stir until combined. Makes about 3 cups tzatziki. Cover and refrigerate until use. It will keep up to 1 week in the refrigerator; any leftover tzatziki makes for a great dip with lightly toasted pita, and also a very solid yogurt-based marinade for garlicky chicken.

For the sandwiches, lightly brush the tops and bottoms of the pita bread with the olive oil. Toast the pita bread on a griddle over medium-high heat until small golden patches appear on the raised area of the pita, about 2 minutes on each side.

Take a pita and lay it flat, bubbly side up. Lay a chicken souvlaki skewer down the center of the pita. Press down on the meat with the flattened palm of your hand and pull the skewer out with one fluid motion, leaving the chicken pieces on the pita. Discard the skewer. Top with ¼ cup shredded lettuce, 2 tablespoons tzatziki, 4 to 6 tomato slices, a light handful of onion slices, ¼ cup feta, and ¼ teaspoon cayenne pepper.

Fold up the edges of the pita around the center so that they just touch over the fillings. Wrap in wax paper and secure with a toothpick. Repeat with the remaining ingredients to make 6 sandwiches and serve immediately.

Tzatziki

1½ cucumbers, peeled

16 ounces plain Greek yogurt

4 garlic cloves, minced

1 tablespoon extra virgin olive oil

1 teaspoon white vinegar

½ teaspoon kosher salt

½ teaspoon freshly cracked black pepper

Chicken Souvlaki Sandwiches

6 quality fluffy pita breads (not pita pockets)

4 teaspoons extra virgin olive oil

6 cooked skewers Chicken Souvlaki (page 115)

1½ cups shredded lettuce

2 medium tomatoes, halved and sliced

1 small red onion, thinly sliced

1½ cups feta cheese stored in brine, drained

1½ teaspoons cayenne pepper

Hawaiian BBQ Pulled Chicken Sandwiches *with Caramelized Pineapple*

Hawaiian BBQ Pulled Chicken

1 cup canned crushed pineapple

¼ cup soy sauce

¼ cup ketchup

3 tablespoons light brown sugar

1 tablespoon water

1 tablespoon mirin

1 tablespoon ponzu

1 tablespoon minced fresh ginger

1 sweet onion, diced

3 cloves minced garlic

1 pound large boneless skinless chicken breasts (about 2)

Caramelized Pineapple

2 tablespoons unsalted butter

4 fresh pineapple rings, about 1 inch thick

1 teaspoon light brown sugar

4 onion buns

THERE ARE JUST SOME WORDS THAT BELONG TOGETHER, and "caramelized" and "pineapple" are two of them. The pineapple is sautéed in butter with a dash of brown sugar until it turns deep golden on both sides, sweet and buttery rings with a toasted sugar aftertaste. These are placed on top of Hawaiian BBQ pulled chicken (from slow-cooking chicken in a pineapple-based barbecue sauce) to create unforgettable tangy-sweet sandwiches that are perfect for any occasion. • serves 4

For the chicken, in a large Dutch oven, mix together the crushed pineapple, soy sauce, ketchup, brown sugar, water, mirin, ponzu, and fresh ginger until combined. Stir in the onion and garlic. Cover and cook over medium heat, stirring every 5 minutes, until the pineapple pieces have softened, 15 to 20 minutes. Add the chicken and reduce the heat to low. Cover and simmer, turning the chicken over once halfway through, for 30 minutes, until the chicken is cooked through. Remove from the heat and pull the chicken meat apart with two forks until the meat is completely shredded. Stir to combine the chicken shreds with the sauce in the pan. Set aside.

For the caramelized pineapple, melt the butter in a large frying pan over medium heat. Sprinkle the pineapple with the brown sugar and cook the pineapple in the pan, stirring occasionally, until golden on each side, 10 to 15 minutes per side.

Evenly distribute the pulled chicken between the four buns and top with a caramelized pineapple ring. Serve immediately.

Pan-Fried Chicken Liver Sandwiches

2 tablespoons all-purpose flour

1 teaspoon minced fresh thyme leaves

¼ teaspoon garlic powder

¼ teaspoon freshly cracked black pepper

½ pound chicken livers, patted dry

2 tablespoons unsalted butter

1 slice thick-cut bacon, cut into ½-inch squares

3 shallots, diced

1 garlic clove, minced

1 tablespoon red wine vinegar

1 tablespoon sherry or brandy

2 tablespoons minced fresh parsley

½ teaspoon kosher salt

8 slices French bread, toasted

THIS SIMPLE BUT DECADENT SANDWICH FILLING combines chicken livers, bacon, shallots, and sherry. The most important part is to not over-cook the livers or they'll become tough and chewy and lose their pleasant texture. The best way to avoid this is to cut them in half every minute once they're browned on the outside until you can see that they're cooked through. Also, using good French bread is a must here, as the rich and buttery filling calls for some seriously fluffy and absorbent bread. • serves 4

In a medium bowl, whisk together the flour, thyme, garlic powder, and black pepper. Add the chicken livers and toss to coat.

Melt the butter in a large pan over high heat. Add the bacon, shallots, and garlic and cook, stirring occasionally, until the shallots have softened, 3 to 5 minutes. Add the livers and cook until lightly browned all over but not cooked completely through, about 4 minutes.

Add the vinegar and sherry and stir to combine. Bring to a simmer and allow the mixture to cook until thickened and the liver is cooked through, about 2 more minutes. Be careful not to overcook the livers, as their texture toughens when overcooked. Remove from the heat and stir in the parsley and salt.

Evenly distribute the liver mixture between four slices of toasted bread. Top with the remaining four slices of bread and serve.

FRENCH ONION–CHICKEN BURGERS

THIS RECIPE COMBINES THE RICH FLAVOR of French onion soup with moist, flavorful chicken burgers. The onions are slowly caramelized in butter and white wine, concentrating the flavor of each. Chicken patties are made with a dash of thyme, garlic powder, and beef bouillon to give them the right earthy, herbal flavor while keeping them nice and tender. When the chicken and onions are topped with a generous melted slice of Gruyère cheese, you have a chicken burger that can put any beef burger to shame. • serves 6

For the caramelized onions, melt the butter in a large frying pan over medium heat. Add the onions, reduce the heat to medium low, and cook, stirring every 5 minutes, until they turn a deep golden color, about 30 minutes. Add the wine and continue cooking, still stirring every 5 minutes, until the onions are deep gold and fragrant, about another 15 minutes. Set aside.

For the chicken burgers, heat a gas grill to medium heat or heat a grill pan over medium heat on the stovetop.

In a medium bowl, mix together the chicken, egg, bread crumbs, olive oil, thyme, garlic powder, salt, black pepper, and bouillon until completely blended. Shape into 6 patties.

Grease the grill grate or grill pan. Grill the patties, lightly brushing the tops with oil then turning a few times, until the internal temperature reaches at least 175°F. Place a cheese slice on each patty during the last 5 minutes of cooking.

Place about 2 heaping tablespoons of the caramelized onions on a brioche bun bottom and place a cooked patty on top. Place 2 more heaping tablespoons of the onions on top of the patty and top with the top bun. Repeat with the remaining ingredients to make 6 burgers and serve immediately.

Caramelized Onions

1 cup (2 sticks) unsalted butter

4 large sweet onions, cut into ½-inch-thick slices

1 cup dry white wine

Chicken Burgers

2 pounds ground chicken

1 large egg, beaten

⅓ cup dried bread crumbs

1 tablespoon extra virgin olive oil, plus extra for brushing

1 tablespoon fresh thyme leaves, or 1 teaspoon dried thyme

1 teaspoon garlic powder

½ teaspoon kosher salt

½ teaspoon freshly cracked black pepper

¼ teaspoon beef bouillon

6 slices Gruyère cheese

6 brioche buns, cut in half horizontally and toasted

SHIITAKE AND SWISS CHICKEN BURGERS

SHIITAKE AND CREMINI MUSHROOMS ARE FINELY CHOPPED and incorporated into a savory chicken patty with delicious sweet-and-sour flavorings like soy sauce, ponzu, and mirin. Ponzu is a salty-sweet citrus-based Japanese sauce, and mirin is a sweet rice wine that is mostly used for cooking. There's also a leaf of kimchi on each burger. Kimchi is a Korean fermented cabbage that packs a bit of heat; think of it as the spicy version of sauerkraut, but with whole cabbage leaves instead of shredded ones. Both of these can be found in the Asian foods aisle of most major grocery stores. They marinate deep into the patty along with fresh garlic, toasted sesame seeds, dill, and ginger to create one intense, umami-flavored burger. • serves 4

Heat the olive oil and 1 tablespoon of the sesame oil in a large frying pan over medium-high heat. Add the shiitake mushrooms, cremini mushrooms, and 1 teaspoon of the soy sauce. Cook, stirring every few minutes, until the mushrooms have darkened slightly and are pleasantly fragrant, about 7 minutes.

Heat a gas grill to medium heat or heat a grill pan over medium heat on the stovetop.

In a medium bowl, mix together the mushroom mixture with the remaining 1 tablespoon sesame oil, remaining 2 teaspoons soy sauce, 1 tablespoon of the ponzu, the ground chicken, bread crumbs, egg, garlic, brown sugar, mirin, sesame seeds, dill, and ginger until thoroughly combined. Divide the mixture into 4 equal parts and form into 4 large patties.

Grill the patties until light grill marks appear on both sides and the patties are cooked through, about 6 minutes per side. Place a slice of Swiss cheese on each patty during the last few minutes of cooking.

In a small bowl, whisk together the mayonnaise, rice vinegar, and remaining ½ teaspoon ponzu. Place a kale leaf on the bottom of each bun, then top each one with a cooked patty and then a leaf of kimchi. Spread the mayonnaise mixture on each top bun and place on the burgers. Serve immediately.

3 tablespoons extra virgin olive oil

2 tablespoons sesame oil

5 ounces shiitake mushrooms, finely diced

2 ounces cremini mushrooms, finely diced

3 teaspoons soy sauce

1 tablespoon plus ½ teaspoon ponzu

1 pound ground chicken

⅔ cup panko bread crumbs

1 large egg

4 garlic cloves, minced

1 tablespoon light brown sugar

1 teaspoon mirin

¼ teaspoon toasted sesame seeds

¼ teaspoon dried dill

¼ teaspoon dried ground ginger

4 slices Swiss cheese

⅓ cup mayonnaise

1 teaspoon rice vinegar

4 plain white poppy seed buns

4 leaves kale, about 4 inches in diameter

4 leaves kimchi, about 4 inches in diameter

CHICKEN SPRING ROLLS *with Peanut Sauce*

Chicken Filling

2 tablespoons vegetable oil

1 pound ground chicken

⅔ cup sliced green onions

½ cup diced shallots

2 tablespoons minced
  lemongrass

¼ cup freshly squeezed lime
  juice

2 tablespoons chopped fresh
  cilantro

1 tablespoon fish sauce

1 to 3 teaspoons chili garlic
  sauce, depending on your
  heat intensity preference

Peanut Sauce

¾ cup full-fat coconut milk

½ cup well-stirred unsweetened
  natural creamy peanut butter

¼ cup granulated sugar

3 tablespoons water

2 tablespoons red Thai curry
  paste

1 tablespoon white vinegar

1¼ teaspoons kosher salt

1 teaspoon chili garlic sauce

Spring Rolls

About 12 round dried rice paper
  wrappers

36 fresh mint leaves

24 fresh Thai basil leaves

12 lettuce leaves, or other
  tender raw green

2 cups freshly cooked rice
  vermicelli noodles, cooled to
  warm

I'M SLIGHTLY OBSESSED WITH THE TEXTURAL SIDE of fresh spring rolls. The wrapper is made up of a delightfully soft and gummy sheet of rice paper, and the filling consists of fresh greens and herbs, rice noodles, and ground chicken. You take the whole thing and dip it in a creamy and rich peanut sauce, so you end up with crunchy veggies, a soft spongy wrapper and noodles, and a warm and thick sauce, covering all the best textural sensations of food. • makes about 12 spring rolls, serving 4

For the chicken filling, heat the vegetable oil in a medium frying pan over medium heat. Add the ground chicken and cook, stirring, until partially cooked, about 6 minutes, breaking it apart with the end of a wooden spoon as it is cooking. Add the green onions, shallots, and lemongrass and continue cooking, stirring occasionally, until the chicken is cooked through and no longer pink. Remove from the heat and drain the excess liquid from the pan. Empty the ground chicken mixture into a bowl and cool to room temperature. Add the lime juice, cilantro, fish sauce, and chili garlic sauce and toss. Set aside.

For the peanut sauce, in a small saucepan, heat all of the ingredients over medium-low heat, whisking constantly. Bring to a simmer and cook until completely smooth, about 3 minutes. Let cool to room temperature.

To assemble the spring rolls, soften one rice paper sheet by dipping it into a large bowl of very warm water and rotating the rice paper constantly for 30 seconds. Place the rice paper on a clean flat surface, such as a plastic cutting board. Arrange 3 of the mint leaves and 2 of the basil leaves in a straight line near the bottom of the circle, leaving about 2 inches of space on each side. Place a lettuce leaf on top of them and then place a few tablespoons of the chicken mixture on top of the lettuce leaf. Top with a small handful of the noodles, still maintaining the 2 inches of empty space on either side of the filling.

Fold the empty sides on either side of the filling inward to partially cover the filling. Tightly roll the rice paper around the filling, beginning at the bottom and rolling towards the top, until sealed. Repeat with the remaining sheets of rice paper and filling to make about 12 spring rolls. Serve immediately along with the peanut sauce for dipping.

Chicken Sumac Wraps *with Beets and Feta*

The slightly sour tang of sumac pairs perfectly with roast chicken, beets, and feta in this comforting wrap. The skin of the chicken thighs turns an appealing golden brown while roasting, and the sugar within the beets caramelizes while their interior softens and their exterior gets delightfully crispy. The chicken and beets are sprinkled with fresh feta cheese before being topped with romaine leaves and rolled up in a spinach tortilla. The crispy, smooth, creamy, and crunchy textures paired with the sweet, savory, and sour flavors make for an especially pleasant wrap. • serves 4

1 teaspoon sumac

1 teaspoon kosher salt

½ teaspoon freshly cracked black pepper

¼ garlic powder

¼ teaspoon cinnamon

¼ teaspoon allspice

1 pound chicken thighs (about 2), bone in and skin on

1 pound beets, peeled and quartered

1 tablespoon extra virgin olive oil

4 large spinach tortillas

3 ounces feta cheese stored in brine, drained

4 to 8 romaine lettuce leaves

Preheat the oven to 400°F.

In a small bowl, mix together the sumac, salt, black pepper, garlic powder, cinnamon, and allspice. Coat the chicken and beets with the olive oil and then the spice mixture. Spread them out on a baking sheet and roast for 45 minutes to 1 hour, until the chicken is cooked through and golden and the beets have wrinkled. Let cool. Remove the chicken meat from the bones and cut into 1-inch pieces, keeping the skin on.

Lay a tortilla flat and place a handful of chicken in the center. Sprinkle roughly 3 tablespoons of the feta cheese over the chicken and place 2 or 3 beet quarters on top of the feta. Top with 1 or 2 romaine lettuce leaves. Fold the two sides of the tortilla over the filling, roll up the tortilla, and place on a serving platter, seam side down. Repeat with the remaining ingredients to make 4 wraps and serve.

ODDS & ENDS

Baked Curry Chicken Cracklings

1 pound chicken skin

¾ teaspoon kosher salt

½ teaspoon dried rosemary

½ teaspoon garlic powder

½ teaspoon curry powder

CRACKLINGS ARE A SOUTHERN APPETIZER that traditionally consists of pork skin that's deep-fried until crispy and puffed. These cracklings are baked rather than fried, which reduces the greasiness that fried cracklings tend to have. It also ensures a nice and crispy crackling—as does scraping off as much of the excess fat from the underside of the skin as possible. This helps dry out the skin while it's baking and makes a nice crunchy chip rather than a chewy one. The baked cracklings are tossed in a garlic and rosemary curry seasoning mixture that makes them even more savory and that much more of an addictive appetizer. But their enjoyment isn't limited to snacking, they also make a great crunchy topping for sandwiches and wraps, and make for a savory gluten-free crouton substitute in salads. This recipe calls for 1 pound of chicken skin, which you can either get from a butcher or acquire through saving and freezing raw chicken skin as you use the meat of the bird. • serves 2

Preheat the oven to 375°F. Line a baking sheet with parchment paper.

Take a piece of chicken skin and lay it flat on the cutting board. Use a blunt knife to scrape the excess fat off the skin. Set the skin aside on a paper towel and repeat until all the chicken skin has been cleaned.

In a small bowl, mix together the salt, rosemary, garlic powder, and curry powder until combined.

Place the chicken skin on the baking sheet, leaving about 1 inch around each piece. Sprinkle with half of the spice mixture. Place another sheet of parchment paper over the chicken skin and another baking sheet on top of it to keep the skin from curling up as it cooks. Bake for about 40 minutes, until the skins are crisp and golden brown, rotating the pan 180 degrees once halfway through cooking.

Use tongs to move the chicken skins to a large plate lined with paper towels to absorb excess oil. Transfer to the serving plate, sprinkle with the remaining spice mixture, and serve.

CRACKLING, BACON, AND ONION JAM

I KNOW THE FOLLOWING INGREDIENTS might sound like something for an old apothecary tonic, but trust me when I tell you that when they combine, they create the king of all jams. Both sweet and savory, this jam can be spread on nearly any type of food. Crackers, bread, meatloaf, cabbage, hamburgers, bagels, cookies…the list could pretty much go on forever. And the best part is that it freezes very well, so you can make several batches, put a few jars of it in the freezer, and spread out your enjoyment over several weeks. • makes one 12-ounce jar

---

1¼ pounds thick-cut bacon

½ pound chicken skin

2 medium yellow onions, thinly sliced

5 garlic cloves, minced

1 bay leaf

½ teaspoon freshly cracked black pepper

¼ teaspoon rubbed dried sage

¼ teaspoon dried savory

½ cup packed light brown sugar

½ cup rice vinegar

½ cup strong brewed coffee

⅓ cup pure maple syrup

¼ cup strong brewed English breakfast tea

Cook the bacon and chicken skin in a large Dutch oven over medium-high heat, stirring every 5 minutes, until the fat is released and the bacon and chicken skin are browned, about 20 minutes.

Remove the bacon and chicken skin with a slotted spoon and set aside on a plate lined with paper towels. Pour the fat from the pot into a jar, leaving 3 tablespoons of the fat remaining in the Dutch oven. Seal the jar with an airtight lid and refrigerate to use for something else.

Return the Dutch oven to medium-high heat. Add the onions, garlic, bay leaf, black pepper, sage, and savory and stir to coat in the fat. Cook, stirring every few minutes, until the onions are translucent and lightly golden around the edges, about 10 minutes.

While the onion mixture is cooking, chop the chicken skin and bacon into roughly 1-inch squares.

Add the brown sugar, vinegar, coffee, maple syrup, and tea to the Dutch oven and mix well. Bring to a rapid boil and cook for 4 minutes. Add the bacon and chicken skin, reduce the heat to low, and simmer, uncovered, until the jam is thick, dark, and syrupy, about 2 hours. Let cool slightly.

Puree in a food processor until a relatively smooth paste forms. Empty the mixture into a 12-ounce Mason jar and let cool to room temperature before sealing and refrigerating. Store for up to 2 weeks in the refrigerator or up to 6 months in the freezer. Can be served chilled, at room temperature, or warm.

Nectarine, Orzo, and Chicken Neck Salad

1 pound chicken necks or backs

¾ cup vegetable stock

½ lemon, cut into 3 slices

2 garlic cloves, thinly sliced

1 sprig fresh dill

2 bay leaves

1 pound orzo pasta

2 ounces feta stored in brine, drained

2 nectarines, cut into 16 wedges

½ large red onion, diced

2 tablespoons freshly squeezed lemon juice

1 tablespoon extra virgin olive oil

1 heaping tablespoon minced fresh dill

½ teaspoon freshly cracked black pepper

Kosher salt to taste

1 tablespoon fresh mint leaves, for garnish (optional)

THE INTENSE, SAVORY FLAVOR OF CHICKEN NECK MEAT contrasts perfectly with fresh juicy nectarines and lemon vinaigrette in this light and refreshing salad. Raw red onion adds a crunchy element of heat, while rich and creamy feta ties it all together. • serves 4

Place the chicken, stock, lemon, garlic, dill, and bay leaves in a small pot and bring to a boil over medium heat. Reduce the heat to low, cover, and simmer until the meat is tender and falls off the bone easily when scraped with a fork, about 1 hour 30 minutes. Let cool slightly. Pick up a piece of chicken and pinch out the meat from between each vertebra with your thumb and forefinger, letting the meat fall back into the pot. Discard the bones. Fish out the bay leaves and lemon rinds from the pot and discard.

Prepare the orzo according to the package directions until al dente. Drain, rinse with cool water to prevent overcooking, and drain again.

In a large bowl, toss the orzo with the chicken mixture, feta, nectarines, onion, lemon juice, olive oil, dill, and black pepper until combined. Taste and add salt and mint leaves as desired. Serve immediately at room temperature or cover and refrigerate for up to 2 hours before serving.

CHICKEN LIVER PÂTÉ

THERE'S NO PUTTING IT LIGHTLY, liver, from any animal, has a very strong and bold flavor. On its own it can be a little overwhelming, but when mixed with butter, brandy, onion, garlic, shallot, and spices, it turns into the most luxurious and flavorful of spreads. The velvety pâté, reminiscent of a plump herb-rubbed roast chicken with an enticing hint of liver, is perfect for spreading on a fresh baguette or set of savory crackers. • serves 8

1½ cups whole milk

¼ cup plus 1 tablespoon brandy

1 pound chicken livers

8 tablespoons (1 stick) unsalted butter

½ large yellow onion, chopped

1 large shallot, diced

1 garlic clove, minced

2 bay leaves

2 teaspoons minced fresh thyme leaves

1 teaspoon minced fresh sage leaves

½ teaspoon kosher salt

½ teaspoon freshly cracked black pepper

Sliced baguette or crackers, for serving

In a large bowl, mix the milk and the 1 tablespoon brandy. Add the chicken livers and toss gently to coat. Cover the bowl and refrigerate for about 1 hour. Drain the livers, discarding the milk.

Melt ¼ cup of the butter in a large frying pan over medium heat. Add the onion, shallot, and garlic and cook, stirring, until the onion begins to look transparent, about 5 minutes. Add the livers and bay leaves and cook, stirring occasionally, until the livers are lightly browned on all sides, about 15 minutes. Add the remaining ¼ cup brandy, the thyme, and sage and bring to a simmer. Allow to cook, uncovered, until the liquid has reduced by half. Let cool for 15 minutes.

Empty the contents of the pot into a high-powered blender or food processor. Add the remaining ¼ cup butter, the salt, and black pepper and blend until a smooth puree forms. Transfer to a serving bowl, cover, and refrigerate for at least 4 hours before serving with a sliced baguette or crackers.

Slow-Cooked Gizzards *with Onion and Lemon*

2 tablespoons extra virgin
   olive oil

1 medium yellow onion, thickly
   sliced

3 garlic cloves, thinly sliced

1 pound chicken gizzards

¼ cup chicken stock

2 tablespoons white wine

½ teaspoon kosher salt

¼ teaspoon freshly cracked
   black pepper

1 tablespoon freshly squeezed
   lemon juice

1 teaspoon minced fresh
   oregano leaves

GIZZARDS ARE AN ADDITIONAL STOMACH ORGAN of the chicken that is used to grind up especially tough seeds and grains. Because this organ is so strong, like the heart, it can be fairly tough in texture when prepared incorrectly. Here, however, it is slow-cooked in onion, garlic, wine, and chicken stock to break down and soften the meat. The savory stew is then drizzled with fresh lemon juice and oregano and served piping hot. The result is a rich and satisfying dish that tastes like good ol' dark meat while being much easier on the wallet. • serves 2

Heat the olive oil in a medium pot over medium-high heat. Add the onion and garlic and cook, stirring every few minutes, until softened and lightly golden around the edges, about 12 minutes.

Add the gizzards, stock, wine, salt, and black pepper. Cover and reduce the heat to low. Simmer until the gizzards are cooked through and have softened slightly, about 1 hour 30 minutes.

Uncover, stir in the lemon juice and oregano, and serve.

POPCORN CHICKEN HEARTS
with Buffalo Sauce and Goat Cheese Dip

THE TOUGH TEXTURE OF CHICKEN HEARTS IS SOFTENED through the deep-frying process: The batter crisps up perfectly on the outside, creating a delicious and affordable batch of popcorn chicken that you wouldn't be able to tell apart from any other dark meat. It's tossed in a spicy homemade buffalo sauce and paired with a creamy goat cheese dip for a little relief from the heat. • serves 4

For the popcorn chicken hearts, add canola oil to a large thick-bottomed pot until it is at least 4 inches deep and at least 4 inches from the top of the pot. Heat the oil until it reaches 350°F.

In a shallow bowl, mix together the milk, eggs, 1 teaspoon of the salt, the garlic powder, and onion powder. In a separate shallow bowl, combine the flour, brown sugar, cayenne pepper, and remaining 1 teaspoon salt.

Dredge the chicken hearts in the flour and shake off the excess. Dip them in the milk mixture and allow the excess to drip off before dredging in the flour a final time. In batches, lower the chicken hearts into the hot oil using a slotted spoon. The temperature will drop to about 325°F once you add the hearts to the oil. Adjust the heat to keep the temperature at 325°F throughout the cooking time. Fry the hearts until golden and cooked through, 8 to 10 minutes. Remove with a slotted spoon and drain on a large platter lined with paper towels. Pat excess oil off with paper towels and let cool while you prepare the sauce and dip.

For the buffalo sauce, melt the butter in a small saucepan over medium heat. Add the hot sauce, chili garlic sauce, honey, onion powder, garlic powder, and paprika and stir to combine. Bring the mixture to a simmer and cook for 2 minutes. Set aside.

For the goat cheese dip, in a small bowl, whisk together the fromage blanc, milk, and black pepper until smooth.

Toss the popcorn chicken hearts in the buffalo sauce in a large bowl until coated. Empty onto a serving platter and serve with the goat cheese dip.

Popcorn Chicken Hearts

Canola oil, for frying

1 cup whole milk

2 large eggs

2 teaspoons kosher salt

½ teaspoon garlic powder

½ teaspoon onion powder

2 cups all-purpose flour

1 tablespoon light brown sugar

1 teaspoon ground cayenne pepper

1 pound chicken hearts

Buffalo Sauce

⅓ cup (⅔ stick) unsalted butter

¼ cup hot sauce of your choosing

¼ cup chili garlic sauce

1 tablespoon honey

1 teaspoon onion powder

½ teaspoon garlic powder

½ teaspoon smoked paprika

Goat Cheese Dip

¼ cup fresh fromage blanc goat cheese

1 tablespoon milk

¼ teaspoon freshly cracked black pepper

CURRIED CHICKEN HEART STIR-FRY

1 tablespoon rice vinegar

2 teaspoons ponzu

1 teaspoon soy sauce

1 teaspoon fish sauce

¼ teaspoon red Thai curry paste

2 tablespoons sesame oil

3 garlic cloves, minced

1 teaspoon grated fresh ginger

1 small yellow onion, sliced

1½ cups broccoli florets

⅔ cup coarsely chopped green beans

⅔ cup sliced shiitake mushrooms

1 pound chicken hearts, cut into thirds lengthwise

1 cup sliced red bell pepper

6 green onions, sliced

CHICKEN HEARTS ARE NEARLY ALL PROTEIN and quite inexpensive, making them a great ingredient for your health and for your budget. The only issue is that they can be relatively tough in texture, but there is a way to break the toughness down. You can cut the hearts into slices, which helps break apart the muscle tissue and allows the meat to cook quickly. They're cooked in a dry Thai curry sauce along with ginger, onion, green beans, broccoli, and mushrooms to create a revitalizing dish that is simmering with flavor and freshness. • serves 2

In a small bowl, whisk together the rice vinegar, ponzu, soy sauce, fish sauce, and curry paste until combined. Set aside.

In a large wok, heat the sesame oil over medium-high heat. Add the garlic and ginger and cook, stirring occasionally, until fragrant, about 2 minutes. Add the onion, broccoli, green beans, and mushrooms and cook, stirring every minute, until the broccoli begins to turn a deep vibrant green, about 5 minutes.

Add the chicken hearts, bell pepper, and curry mixture and stir to combine. Cook, stirring every minute, until the chicken hearts are just cooked through, 4 to 5 minutes. Remove from the heat and toss with the green onions. Serve immediately.

FRIED CHICKEN FEET

MOST PEOPLE MAY BALK AT THE IDEA of eating chicken feet, but the chewy texture is made more enjoyable when fried because the exterior develops a wonderful crunch (think calamari). I use a bit of cayenne here to pack some heat into the dish, but if you prefer a milder version you can always cut out the cayenne and double the amount of paprika. • serves 2

1 pound chicken feet

1½ teaspoons kosher salt

1 teaspoon garlic powder

½ teaspoon ground cayenne pepper

½ teaspoon paprika

½ teaspoon onion powder

½ teaspoon freshly cracked black pepper

2 cups all-purpose flour

2 large eggs

Canola oil, for frying

Bring a large pot of water to a boil over high heat. Add the chicken feet and cook for about 8 minutes, skimming the scum that forms on top with a mesh spoon and discarding it. Drain the chicken feet in a colander and immediately rinse with cold water. Pat dry and use kitchen shears to cut off the ends of the toes where the claws begin. Discard the chicken claws and reserve the feet. Allow the feet to dry completely on a wire rack lined with paper towels.

In a small bowl, mix together the salt, garlic powder, cayenne, paprika, onion powder, and black pepper. Combine half of the spice mixture with the flour in a shallow bowl and mix until combined. Beat the eggs in a second shallow bowl.

Add canola oil to a large pot until the oil is 4 inches deep and at least 4 inches from the top of the pot. Heat the oil until it reaches 350°F.

Dip the feet in the eggs, shaking off any excess, and dredge in the flour mixture to coat. In batches, add to the oil and fry until deeply golden, 4 to 6 minutes. Remove using tongs and let cool for a few minutes on a wire rack lined with paper towels. Sprinkle the fried chicken feet with the remaining spice mixture and serve.

Roasted Sesame Chicken Feet

1 tablespoon sesame oil

1 tablespoon crushed dried red
   pepper flakes

1 teaspoon fish sauce

1 teaspoon light brown sugar

1 teaspoon sweet dark soy sauce

½ teaspoon soy sauce

½ teaspoon garlic powder

1½ pounds chicken feet,
   declawed

THE DISTINCTLY CHEWY TEXTURE OF CHICKEN FEET is lessened by a good roast in the oven, creating a nice and crispy exterior. They're coated in a spicy, sweet, and savory sauce, creating an addicting snack with deeply layered flavors and a very low price tag. • serves 3

———————————————

Preheat the oven to 425°F.

In a large bowl, whisk together the sesame oil, pepper flakes, fish sauce, brown sugar, dark sweet soy sauce, soy sauce, and garlic powder until combined. Add the chicken feet and toss to coat. Spread the chicken feet out on a baking sheet in an even layer and roast until darkened and crispy, 30 to 40 minutes.

INDEX